The

EVERYTHING®
Negotiating Book

Dear Reader:

Wouldn't our daily challenges be better met if we had the right tools at the right time at our disposal? Well, good news! You already have the fundamental skills required for negotiating! I want you to feel comfortable using them, whether you're buying a car, trying to get your credit card interest rates reduced, or hoping to get compensation for an item you bought and are not happy with. I encourage you to use this book as your most indispensable tool for honing your skills and making them work for you.

Everyone can benefit from learning how to master the art of negotiating—teachers who need to make their case for buying needed classroom supplies, parents who'd like to find a better way to handle conflicts with their children, and professionals who need to brush up for their next meeting. However you choose to use this book, the fact that you're holding it in your hand means you have a desire to learn about how negotiating fits into your life.

Keep reading—you're about to find out!

Angelique Pinet

The EVERYTHING® Series

Editorial

Publishing Director	Gary M. Krebs
Managing Editor	Kate McBride
Copy Chief	Laura MacLaughlin
Acquisitions Editor	Gina Marzilli
Development Editor	Julie Gutin
Production Editor	Jamie Wielgus
	Bridget Brace

Production

Production Director	Susan Beale
Production Manager	Michelle Roy Kelly
Series Designers	Daria Perreault
	Colleen Cunningham
	John Paulhus
Cover Design	Paul Beatrice
	Matt LeBlanc
Layout and Graphics	Colleen Cunningham
	Rachael Eiben
	Michelle Roy Kelly
	John Paulhus
	Daria Perreault
	Erin Ring
Series Cover Artist	Barry Littmann

Visit the entire Everything® Series at www.everything.com

THE
EVERYTHING
NEGOTIATING
BOOK

Savvy techniques for getting what
you want—at work and at home

Angelique Pinet

Adams Media
Avon, Massachusetts

I'd like to dedicate this book to Lesley Bolton, a great and talented friend,
for her endless support, generous spirit, and much-needed laughter.

An Everything® Series Book.
Everything® and everything.com® are registered trademarks of F+W Publications, Inc.

Published by Adams Media, an F+W Publications Company
57 Littlefield Street, Avon, MA 02322 U.S.A.
www.adamsmedia.com

ISBN: 1-59337-152-7

Printed in the United States of America.

J I H G F E D C B A

Library of Congress Cataloging-in-Publication Data
Pinet, Angelique.
The everything negotiating book / Angelique Pinet.
p.   cm.
(An everything series book.)
ISBN 1-59337-152-7
1. Negotiation in business--Handbooks, manuals, etc.
2. Negotiation--Handbooks, manuals, etc. I. Title. II. Series: Everything series.
HD58.6.P56   2005
658.4'052--dc22   2004019142

This book is available at quantity discounts for bulk purchases.
For information, call 1-800-872-5627.

Contents

Acknowledgments

It takes a lot of perseverance for an author to make it through the abundance of rejection letters she receives until finally someone takes notice and gives her the opportunity of a lifetime. For this, I am grateful to Gina Marzilli, who had the courage to trust in my abilities and the patience to guide me through it.

I am also thankful to Julie Gutin for going above and beyond the call of duty to make this book possible and for doing it with creative genius.

Top Ten Negotiations of Your Life

1. **Accepting a job offer:** Getting a job offer is very exciting because it means your skills are in demand. But before you sign the offer, see if you can negotiate for a higher salary or more vacation days!

2. **Buying a car:** Now that you have a great job, you'll need to find a way to get there. It's going to take more than courage to step on that car lot, so sharpen your skills!

3. **Buying a house:** You'll need to take your negotiating experience to the next level because this negotiation requires you to deal with several different people along the way.

4. **Purchasing furniture:** Of course you'll need to fill your new house with lots of new furniture. Because this can get expensive, you'll want to learn how to be a competent negotiator to get the best prices.

5. **Choosing a computer:** Negotiate for the best software package, most up-to-date features, and best warranty on the market.

6. **Negotiating a raise:** You've been working hard, and you've acquired a lot of expenses since you first accepted the job offer. Building a strong case before asking your boss for a raise can help you get the money you deserve.

7. **Planning your wedding:** Before you can declare your love and head off into the sunset together, be prepared for a series of negotiations that will make your big day perfect.

8. **Starting a business:** This is a giant step in your career, and it involves a lifetime of negotiations that will require impeccable deal-making abilities.

9. **Going through a divorce:** This is one negotiation no one wants to have to make. It requires a lot of emotional restraint and unfailing focus.

10. **Making a will:** To make sure everything you spent your life working for ends up in the right hands, this is one document you'll need to spend a lot of time preparing.

Introduction

▶ How many times have you felt like you should have gotten a better deal on something but didn't know how to do it? How many times have you had the feeling that you paid too much for something because you had no other choice? If you're like most people, you've been there and done that more than you'd like to admit.

If you cringe at the very thought of having to negotiate, you are not alone. You probably envision long hours of haggling with an unpleasant salesperson and getting nowhere in the process. True, negotiating can be an exhausting event at times, but for the most part it isn't as dreadful as you think. In fact, you negotiate all the time—successfully! From accepting a job offer to participating in work-related meetings to hashing out the details of a child's curfew, you've been putting your skills to the test all along!

But it doesn't stop there. As a consumer, you negotiate your budget on a regular basis to determine what you want versus what you can afford. As a homeowner you negotiate with many people, like pest exterminators and landscapers. As a spouse, you negotiate sharing household responsibilities and tasks.

You see, negotiating isn't always about price. The process permeates many different parts of your life and can help you in more ways than you can imagine. To be a good negotiator, you have to educate yourself—it'll help you discuss the matter with your opponent and make the right decisions. And it can certainly improve your organizational skills so that you never leave the important details out and you always have the information you need when you need it.

The art of negotiating teaches you how to present your case to others in a way that helps them understand your side of things. You learn how to gain a good amount of control in situations instead of leaving yourself vulnerable. More importantly, you learn that it's okay to ask for the things you want. I spent two taxing hours with a salesman trying to buy a laptop computer one day. When the deal was finished, he asked if there was anything else I needed at that time. When I replied that I had planned on buying a laptop carrying case but was too frustrated to spend any more money, he told me to pick one out and he'd throw it in as part of the deal because I had been so patient with him through it all. It truly never hurts to ask for what you want.

Like any game, once you learn the fundamental skills required to play and figure out what you're up against, you can relax and have fun. One of the basic skills of negotiating is learning how to study your opponent. Figuring out how to read body language and facial expressions is a skill you can use anywhere. After all, we interact with people every day, and it's a lot easier to do that when we can understand how they communicate and what they are trying to say. The tips in this book will help you fend off the forceful salesperson and hold your own against a pushy coworker. It also gives you insight into your own character so you can find your weakest spots and guard against them.

As you begin your journey into the adventure of negotiating, forget everything you thought you knew about it, and open your mind to all the wonderful things the process has to offer. Once you have a look around, you'll realize how gratifying it is to possess the skills necessary for success. Simply let the pages of this book be your guide into that fascinating world, and discover the many ways you can apply what you've learned to the things that are happening in your life right now.

Chapter 1

The Settlement Game

You've been playing it all your life, but you just haven't realized it yet. Who knew all those days of trading baseball cards and exchanging Mom's turkey sandwich for a more delectable snack were nature's funny way of preparing you for adulthood? Sure, it was easier and more simplified when you weren't aware that you were negotiating. However, tapping into the core skills you developed during all those lunchtime scrimmages is easy once you learn where your innate desire to "swap" originated.

Bartering Back Through Time

No one knows when the first barter took place, but we do know that bartering has been around for much longer than buying and selling. During simpler times when you couldn't just get in your car and drive to the nearest Wal-Mart to purchase anything your heart desired, a system of give-and-take accommodated anyone who chose to participate. Whether it was to acquire a piece of lamb in exchange for some pottery or to obtain jewelry for a hand-painted headpiece, people were finding ways to fulfill their needs.

Bartering is an exchange of goods or services where money isn't involved. The worth of the objects or services being exchanged is up to the two parties involved, and establishing exact worth is where negotiation comes in.

Bartering was a way to acquire life's necessities, but it was more than that—it was a way to break the barriers of communication. When people met for the first time, bartering was a way to observe if the person was trustworthy and genuine, and only after mutual willingness to trade was expressed would a dialogue between the two parties ensue. (This is equally true today in many cultures.)

Bartering didn't have to be immediate—the exchange could take place at two different points of time. For example, when guests visited someone's home, they brought along gifts as a sign of respect and gratitude. Later, when the guests departed, the host would give them something of his own to take with them for the journey home.

Eventually, bartering slowly evolved into a primitive financial arrangement, in which cows, sheep, and other livestock were used as one of the first forms of currency. Plants, produce, and other agricultural items also served as currency, only to be overtaken by precious metals, stones, and finally paper bills.

FACT

Cowries—marine snails boasting thick, glossy shells peppered with tiny flecks—appeared in China in 1200 B.C. as the first objects to be used as money. They were widely used, and even became popular in faraway places like Africa, where some cultures continue to exchange them today. Cowries are the longest used currency in history.

From Bargaining to Negotiating

When people bartered, most of the time they knew the values of the objects they exchanged. Let's say that three baskets of corn were generally worth one chicken. Two parties had to persuade each other to go through with the exchange, but they didn't have to worry about setting the price. But what if one year there was a drought and there wasn't much corn to go around? Then maybe a farmer with three baskets of corn could bargain to exchange them for two or even three chickens. Bargaining the exchange value of something is one form of negotiating. And it works once you switch to a currency system.

The way people bargain with each other varies from culture to culture, but you've seen it before at your local yard sale or flea market. The vendor gives you a price, you give the vendor a price, and eventually either a happy medium is decided upon or you walk away. More often than not, the vendor inches down on her price while you inch up on your price, until you're both at a number that doesn't allow either one of you to budge any more!

A different type of bargaining can be seen at your local auction, where a roomful of people view the items up for sale and make their bids on the items they wish to buy. If someone outbids them, they're then given the opportunity to up their bid. This continues back and forth until one person has outbid all interested parties. Today, millions of people search for, post, trade, barter, bid, and buy anything from toys they had as children to signed sports paraphernalia on eBay and other Internet auction sites. If only our sheep-trading ancestors could see us now!

Bargaining the Price

While the terms "bargaining" and "negotiating" are synonymous, there's a distinct difference between the two. Bargaining involves streamlining wants and needs into a single focus. Before you ever step foot on the lawn where your neighbor's yard sale is taking place, you know in your mind that all the handwritten sticker prices are not permanent. Your goal is to get the item you desire at the lowest price possible. Your neighbor's goal on the other hand, is twofold—she wants to get rid of as many items as possible, and she wants to get the most amount of money for them.

Whenever you're shopping at a yard sale, always ask the seller what the price of the item is. If the seller responds with a question of her own—how much do you want to pay for it?—don't give up. Instead, insist on getting a price quote. Of course, when you're on the selling end, get the customer to give you a price. If it's too low you can turn it down, but if it's higher than what you had in mind, congratulate yourself!

When it comes to bargaining, everyone's focus is limited and all efforts are spent trying to get the best deal—for themselves. In this case, money is the focal point, and that's when the price war begins: "How much?" "A dollar." "I'll give you fifty cents." "Eighty cents." "Sixty cents." "Seventy cents." "Sixty-five cents." "Deal."

When a goal becomes concentrated, it's easy to lose sight of what's really important. In the yard-sale example, price takes precedence over the usefulness of the product. The purchaser never stops to think, "If I thought it was worth only fifty cents a minute ago, why do I think it's worth more now?" Although the settled price was split equally down the middle, one person spent more than they intended to and the other person received less money for the item than they hoped to receive. So who got the bargain?

Some people are said to "drive a hard bargain," meaning there's little to no chance of swaying them away from believing their offer is fair. You can't bargain with them—they are convinced that they know best or that there's someone out there who'll pay the full price. Thus, the department-store mentality is born, and the only way you're ever paying a lower price is if there's a sale.

Negotiating a Deal

Negotiating is the art of agreeing on something or settling a question between two parties. Although it may involve bartering or settling on a price, more often than not people negotiate a deal on how to behave toward each other.

A good negotiation draws on the skills used for marketplace bartering and on the focused determination required of bargaining. Negotiating encompasses a wide range of core principles and becomes a series of plays that you must know how and when to use throughout the entire game. In addition to remaining focused and forging strong relationships, you'll need to be informed, be prepared, know who your challengers are, and have other alternatives.

Although there are several types of negotiation that will be discussed in this book, the two most common are positional negotiating and win/win negotiating. The former is when neither side moves from its original position because both are so focused on their own needs that they cannot even begin to comprehend the other party's needs. A power struggle ensues; goals and objects are never discussed, resulting in hours of trying to produce agreements that everyone is satisfied with; long-term relationships are jeopardized because there's too much negativity being exhibited. Everyone is out for himself, and that's it.

The only way to avoid falling into the positional negotiating trap is to adopt a win/win strategy, in which both parties have their needs met. This way, mutual agreements can be made more easily. To be successful at win/win negotiating, it's important to figure out what everyone else's needs are and make one's own needs flexible so everyone is willing to play fair. Decisions are reached more quickly, great strides are made toward building positive relationships, and everybody is happy when it comes time to walk out of the room.

Win/win negotiating is successful because everyone goes into it with a positive attitude, a firm understanding of how the game is played, and a professional approach to the situation at hand. This book promotes win/win negotiating and will continually illustrate the steps that make it such a gratifying way to do business.

The Benefits Are Evident

There are endless reasons why negotiations can be beneficial, and most of them have their roots deeply planted in the soil of our bartering ancestor's back yard. Aside from the obvious reasons why negotiations are used in the business world (to increase profit, to form large corporations by merging small businesses, to build reputations), the successes you can achieve on a smaller scale in your personal life carry just as much weight as those achieved by companies through their representatives.

You practice the art of negotiation every day—at the grocery store and the electronics store; with your utility companies, car insurance company, family, friends, and coworkers. If you think you might be a little late with your water bill payment because it happens to fall on the same day you closed on your house, then you might call the utility company to request the date of payment be pushed back. If the bakery at your grocery store carries packages of eight dinner rolls when you only need two, you might ask the clerk to take two out of the bag and price them accordingly. In both situations, you're asking the company you regularly do business with for a concession. What you offer in return is your continued business and a positive opinion about the company's devoted services.

In effect, if two or more people have goals they can help each other reach, they enter into a negotiation. Carpooling allows drivers to conserve gas mileage, limit the amount of wear and tear on their vehicles, and save on the cost of gas. Babysitting usually requires a teenager to forfeit her Saturday night, but it also gives her spending money for next weekend.

What is a concession?

A concession is when you yield to another person by giving him a privilege that you don't usually give to other people. For example, during a business meeting, an executive asks for a 10-percent cut in production costs. The other executive agrees to this concession, but she asks for one of her own in return—that products be delivered a month earlier than usual.

When They Don't Want to Play

Since negotiations require two or more people (unless you're negotiating with yourself on why you should get out of bed when the alarm goes off at 5 A.M.), what do you do if the person you want to negotiate with refuses your offer? First, find out why. There may be a simple explanation. Maybe the person doesn't have the time to take you up on your offer just yet but would be willing to work with you at a later date.

If you can't find out why, find out what. What can you put forth in order to make your proposal more attractive? If the coworker you carpool with decides she likes the freedom of having her own car every day, remind her of the benefits that carpooling provides. You could even offer to let her take your car to lunch or to run errands. By switching the focus on how the deal gives her an advantage, and by giving her something in return for the freedom she'd be giving up, she's more likely to agree to the terms.

When You Don't Want to Play

If an offer has been presented to you and you're not interested, keep in mind that you should never feel pressured to be involved in a negotiation. People usually enter into them with specific goals in mind, so if you just don't understand how a particular deal can work for you, decline it. If this is a deal you'd like to be a part of, but you don't like what's being offered to you, find a way to offer up something the other party wants in exchange for something you want. Remember, part of negotiating involves building relationships, so take advantage of any opportunity that presents itself to you.

The Players

Everyone negotiates. Parents negotiate with teachers; husbands negotiate with wives; brothers negotiate with sisters; defense attorneys negotiate with prosecuting attorneys. Even children exercise a form of negotiating. It's funny how adults are still playing the game of "I'll trade you this for that," only in a more sophisticated and refined manner.

Negotiating for Business

The men and women whose professional expertise is put to use day in and day out perfect the art of negotiating. Bridges are built, roads are repaired, high-rises are erected, public transportation is rerouted, and streets are named—and all the while, there's a group of professionals negotiating the details of these projects by presenting their ideas and strategies to the appropriate board of directors. Every city within every state vies for a piece of the budget, and the way to get it begins with a group of people who are trained to negotiate. Though most careers involve some negotiating aspects, here are a few professions that will really put your skills to the test:

- Lawyer
- Mediator
- Politician
- Business planner
- Editor
- CEO
- Buyer

If you're not sure you have what it takes to be a great negotiator, study this book, and then try putting your newly acquired skills to use. You can start small at first, for example by negotiating the use of one of your company's conference rooms at a certain time and day (even if it's just to throw someone a surprise birthday party). Then, as you start to feel more confident, you can tackle more complicated situations, like renegotiating your salary and benefits. To hone your negotiating skills even further, you can also attend one of the seminars or workshops that are listed in the back of this book in Appendix C.

Negotiating for Personal Reasons

Those creatures of the business world aren't the only ones around here negotiating for a living. If you've ever been a parent, you probably have fond memories of all the wonderful ways your children have tried to get you to give them what they want. And you can probably recall all the deals you made with them in order to get them to clean their rooms or eat their dinner!

ALERT!

While making deals with your children is a great way to get them to do what you ask of them, too much deal-making can have an adverse effect. They start expecting you to always offer a reward in return for something they should be doing as part of their daily chores or personal responsibilities.

In addition to negotiating with children, you may have to come to agreement with other members of your family. These are great moments to utilize your negotiating skills because you have the advantage of feeling comfortable around your family.

Also start paying attention to the encounters you have with salespeople, waiters, hosts, and coworkers. Be especially aware of any requests you made and how successful you were at having them fulfilled.

Timing Is Everything

Timing is the quarterback of negotiating—you have to wait for the right time to throw the ball at the right moment to the right person with the right amount of speed and at the right distance. In fact, timing is so important that an entire chapter of this book has been devoted to it.

One of the most important things to remember about timing is that all parties involved have their own deadlines. Everyone wants to make sure his issues are being discussed and resolved, so some negotiators might try to manipulate time by causing unnecessary delays or by trying to rush the other party into making a quick decision. These tactics should not be tolerated and must be brought up and discussed as soon as they appear.

When the Time Is Right

The time to negotiate is right when you have a well-thought out plan in place and a list of goals you hope to achieve. Steps you've taken ahead of time should include researching your opponent, figuring out you're opponent's wants and needs, preparing to suggest alternatives, knowing what your limits are, and making sure you are aware of any tactics that may be used against you.

Never begin negotiations if you are not prepared or have not done extensive research into what will be discussed and the people you will be meeting with. If it helps, do a few practice runs with friends or family and seek the advice of a lawyer (depending on the severity of the situation).

Respecting the situation of the other party involved in the negotiations gives them time to reconfigure new information, shows character and professionalism, and—most importantly—sets the groundwork for positive relationships and honest business dealings in the future.

Have Patience

While you want to be wary of intentional delays, it is also important to have patience, and lots of it. During the full course of a negotiation period— which can take hours, days, months, or even years, depending on the situation—new concessions, problems, concerns, questions, and ideas will come about, and you will need to have the patience to analyze them thoroughly. Since the purpose of negotiating is to come to an agreement that both parties are satisfied with, give the other party (and yourself) enough time to absorb all of the latest information and to formulate decisions based on the new developments.

Feeling tired or weak? Take a break. Walk out of the room and step outside into the fresh air. Drink something cold and grab a snack to restore your energy. By giving your brain the opportunity to recharge, you can walk back into the meeting room feeling alert and ready to continue with the discussion.

What Is Negotiable?

Simply put, anything is negotiable if you are willing to invest your time and effort in it. As soon as you place value on something, you determine whether it's worth fighting for. Think about who you might negotiate with, and you'll see lots of things that are usually negotiated. You negotiate with bankers, car salespersons, real-estate agents, sellers, vendors, credit card companies, managers, customer-service representatives, neighbors, family, and friends.

A good price, reasonable deadline, forgiveness of a late fee, or help with babysitting might be on a quick list of the kinds of things you can negotiate for. Whether negotiating for a car or for the last piece of apple pie, each experience should sharpen your skills a little more and prepare you for more negotiating to come.

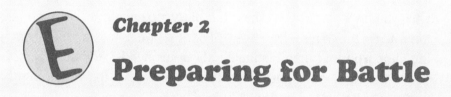

Chapter 2

Preparing for Battle

Now that you're ready to play the game of negotiation, let's see how it's done. Like any good player, it's important to have an all-inclusive understanding of your sport in order to keep your awareness sharp and your advantage strong. Preparation is essential to keeping your head above water; information is your life support. This chapter guides you through the process of doing thorough research so you'll always know whom you're playing, how you're playing, and what you're playing for.

Know Yourself and Your Goals

The first thing you should do before you begin your research is figure out what you want. Organizing your thoughts will give you direction and purpose, and the true focus of your plan will come into view. You should never walk into a negotiation unsure of what you're doing there or not quite decided on what you hope to achieve. The other party, potentially a seasoned negotiator, will use this to his advantage by taking a dominant standpoint and making the purpose of the meeting all about his needs. Additionally, because you're unsure about what's important to you, you'll have nothing to arm yourself with when he hurls a deluge of concessions at you.

To figure out exactly what your goals are, begin by asking yourself the following questions:

- What do I hope to achieve?
- Why are these achievements important to me?
- What is my main goal?
- What are my secondary goals?
- What steps do I need to take to be successful?
- What can prevent me from being successful?
- What am I prepared to do to overcome the obstacles?

List all the goals you hope to achieve, even if some are direct results of others. Next, identify your main goal. Write it out simply and clearly, as it is the primary reason for the strategy you will develop. Bringing your goals to the forefront is only the first step in the process of understanding your objectives. Prioritizing goals and devising a plan for reaching them will give you a deeper understanding of what you need to accomplish during the negotiation.

Prioritizing Your Goals

Your main goal should be the impetus of your entire argument. If you want to buy a car because you need a way to get to work every morning, your main goal is to buy a reliable vehicle. Secondary goals will include whether you want a new or used automobile; whether you prefer a truck, an SUV, or a sedan; and if you want to buy or lease, what color you prefer, the features you're looking for, reasonable price, and so on. It's easier to jot down your goals first and prioritize them later, so you're not leaving anything out.

Set realistic goals. If a goal is too far out of reach, you may feel like you failed if it's not accomplished, when in reality the goal just wasn't easily attainable. Another way to avoid feeling like a loser is to be as specific as possible with your goals so you can track your progress toward achieving them.

Consider Possible Concessions

As you're defining goals, keep in mind that the ability to be flexible may serve to your advantage at some point during the negotiation. While you don't want to easily give up any of your goals, you do want to keep an open mind about how you can adjust them if it means a mutual agreement can be reached.

As mentioned earlier, concessions are privileges—tiny pieces of gold that need to be rationed wisely. Throughout the course of every negotiation, both parties will ask for one concession in exchange for another. Each party wants to walk out of the room feeling satisfied with the concessions that were agreed upon. If you did your homework—researched, prepared, practiced, and weighed alternatives—you should have a good idea of what concessions you're comfortable making.

When you make concessions during negotiations, here are some guidelines to keep in mind:

- Know how to present concessions, from least to most important. Getting the easy ones out of the way first allows you to direct the bulk of your time and energy to more important ones.

- Exhibit the same amount of resistance for every concession so the other party can't tell which concessions have more value to you and which ones do not. You never want the other party to feel like you've gotten more out of her than she's gotten out of you. Otherwise, she's likely to ask for a lot more concessions.
- For every concession you make, ask for one in return. For example, "I'll give you a discount if you make a higher down payment."
- Provide reasons for your concessions so the other party can understand where you're coming from. For example, "I'd like a discount on the sticker price to be able to afford the monthly payments." You'll earn the other party's respect if you prove you're not asking for something just to see if you can get it.

Some experts believe you should always make the first concession. That way you retain control over the ones that are important to you. But others feel that letting the other party make the first concession allows you to take the prize if they overbid. Eventually, you'll develop your own style of negotiating, but for now go with what feels most comfortable to you. Tactics like these (and many more) will be discussed later in this book.

Know Your Limitations

Everyone has limits—and you should, too. Knowing yours before you enter into a negotiation helps you stay focused on what's important and allows you to determine whether the agreement is acceptable. The course of a negotiation often changes, and new concessions and limitations have to be established. When this happens, you'll need to determine if your old limitations still apply.

ALERT!

Don't let the other party know what your limitations are—at least not right away. Making them privy to this information up front might make you seem confrontational and uncompromising. However, if the other party is coming dangerously close to your limits, feel free to warn them that you don't plan to compromise on those particular issues.

So what kinds of limits should you set? Like goals, limits should be flexible but steadfast. Think of them as your bodyguards, ready to protect you on a dime. As soon as you start feeling uncomfortable and things aren't going your way, call attention to your bodyguards so the other party knows they're about to lose your business.

In order to set limits, you should first examine your alternatives. If you could walk away from a negotiation and still have several opportunities waiting, you can be pretty liberal with what limits you set. That's why it can't be stressed enough: Be sure to have other alternatives before you enter into a negotiation. It's also good to know what alternatives the other party has lined up since this will determine the importance they place on their concessions.

Know Your Opponent

Your underlying strategy should be largely based on your negotiating opponent. Study your opponent's playing style, and learn as much as possible about why she's investing her time in the negotiation. By reviewing the other party's training, accomplishments, education, and work history, for example, you can better predict what her actions will be and therefore be more prepared to address them.

Try to get the specifics of what the other party's goals are so you can weigh your leverage against theirs and adjust your game plan if you need to. It's also a good idea to use the first few minutes of the meeting to discuss some of the objectives you share and those that you do not.

It's a Question of Authority

When you prepare to deal with your opponent, consider how much leeway he has to make concessions and compromise. Is this person really authorized to make decisions, or is he merely a proxy for his manager and unable to make decisions on his own?

Whether you're negotiating with one person or five people, directly ask the participants one by one if they are authorized to negotiate with you and to make and agree to concessions. If you're negotiating with only one person and the answer is no, you will have saved yourself hours of wasted time by asking this important question up front. As soon as the other party reveals he is not authorized to make any deals with you, start packing your briefcase and ask if it would be possible to meet with the person who is authorized to negotiate.

A Background Check

Learn as much as you can about the other party's background. One of the most effective ways is to learn about how successful (or unsuccessful) he's been in other negotiations. Talk to anyone you know who's had business dealings with him. Visit the company he works for and look around. What kind of place is it? Are people generally relaxed or on edge? Although this is not a definite indicator of what he'll be like in person, it can be helpful when trying to put together a general profile of his work habits in an effort to forecast his negotiating style.

QUESTION?

What does it mean to "Google" someone?
The Internet is a remarkable tool for finding out anything about anyone anywhere in the world. To "Google" someone, visit ✐*www.google.com* and type the person's name in the search field (for an exact match, put the name in quotation marks). You will get a list of Web sites where that name appears.

Concrete information, like finding out about a person's negotiating style, may prove to be more helpful to you than abstract assumptions. Simply asking the other party a few open-ended questions before negotiations begin can give you some idea of whom you're dealing with. Though you can't assume the answers you receive are 100-percent accurate, asking questions like "How long have you been with the company?"; "How long have you been in your current position?"; and "What do you hope to gain from this negotiation?" indicate, to some extent, the possibility of a hidden agenda. If the other party has been with the company for only three months, then she may be eager to prove herself to her superiors and try to exhibit an aggressive attitude. On the other hand, if the person you're negotiating with has held her position with the company for over fifteen years, she's bound to have a few tricks up her sleeves.

Background Information

Arriving at a negotiation meeting without any notes, research findings, or information of any kind is like a football team going to their game without any of their coaches. If you view the vast amount of resources available to you as your own personal team of coaches, you'll realize why you need them. Coaches offer you a wealth of data, perspectives, options, and useful information—all of which contributes to the success of your strategy. If you do nothing else before negotiations begin, delve into the contents of libraries, online journals, newspapers, and bookstores and ferret out every bit of knowledge they have to offer. Train yourself to be an expert on business dealings, product value, market comparisons, strategies, tactics, practices, and anything else pertinent to your situation, be it buying your first home, a used car, or paint for the exterior of your garage.

Use the Library

Libraries (yes, they still exist) continue to be the best resource for conducting general research. Volumes of information that you simply cannot find on the Internet are available to you every day of the week, and there are librarians who will be glad to help you find what you're looking for. One advantage of going to the library is that you have unlimited access to hundreds of encyclopedias, newspapers, magazines, books, and periodicals. If you were to try to gain access to any of these resources online, you'd most likely be prompted with a window that says you must pay for a subscription in order to have access.

If a book turns up in your search that isn't available at your library, check with the librarian to see if she can have it sent from another location from anywhere in the state. This service is one your tax dollars probably pay for, so you should certainly take advantage of it.

Libraries are a great place to find information about any of the companies you may be doing business with, as well as for looking up a few relative laws you may have been wondering about. This is particularly useful when negotiating a divorce, trying to make a decision on which real estate company to employ, or investigating a series of nursing homes to find the best one for your family member. Also, the validity of the information you find at the library tends to be more trustworthy than most of what's available online.

Probe the Internet

Though you can't always believe what you read or what's uncovered by a Google search, the Internet is the place to go for quick fixes of information. Web sites ending in ".org", ".edu", and ".gov" are usually a safe bet for accurate, up-to-date information. However, there are hundreds of other Web sites that can be of service to you if you just know where to look.

Start visiting popular newspaper Web sites, particularly those that represent major metropolises. There are some business magazines and journals that don't require a subscription to read their contents, and they usually provide several links to other related Web sites you might find useful. Check out Appendix C for a list of free Web sites that offer invaluable tips on negotiating.

Get Firsthand Experience

Nothing prepares you for a situation quite like the way hands-on experience does. Don't be afraid to get your hands dirty! If you know you want to buy a car some time in the near future, visit a few different dealerships and talk to a variety of salespersons. This will give you exposure to their world as well as an up-close look at the kinds of tactics they employ and what types of questions they'll ask you. Study the tones of their voices and what information they choose to share with you.

If your daughter has been hinting around that she'd love for you to get her a new stereo system for her sixteenth birthday, prepare yourself ahead of time by visiting brick-and-mortar stores to look at what's available. If you want to know what the hottest stereo system is (the one all your daughter's friends are buying), visit the same stores frequently and take note of which models are collecting dust as opposed to which models seem to be flying off the shelves every week. Chances are, if everyone else loves it, your daughter will too.

FACT

If a salesman doesn't approach you as soon as you step onto the car lot, more times than not he still knows you're there. He's deliberately waiting to approach you because he wants to monitor the way you look at the product. If he notices you're looking at the tires first, for instance, he'll walk over to you and mention something about the extended warranty their tires carry.

Common and Conflicting Objectives

If you enter into a negotiation with the right mindset, you'll indeed be thinking of ways to make the deal work for both you and the other party. This way of thinking not only builds positive relationships with the people you're working with, but it almost guarantees everyone will be walking away from the table smiling. Before any concessions are made, discuss what objectives you both share and analyze the specific details of the steps that need to be taken to reach those objectives. Brainstorm to develop other solutions that neither one of you had thought of on your own. By focusing on the objectives you both have in common, you're streamlining your combined resources to reach a positive outcome.

Once you've settled the objectives you and the other party have in common, talk about the different objectives you have. Something you deem extremely valuable might be something the other person doesn't consider quite so precious; therefore, he has no problem agreeing to make it work for you. Likewise, the concessions you regard as inconsequential are an important part of the other party's agenda and will not hurt you to give up. Allowing each other to have gains that don't require painful losses on either side is an essential part of the game that should never be overlooked.

Analyze Your Alternatives

Having one or several alternative courses of action is key to having an advantage. You need to be aware that if the negotiation doesn't work out with the current party, you can turn to others. Alternatives provide you with the confidence to reject offers and to walk away from the negotiation if you're not happy with the way it's going. This is where your power comes from, folks, so use it when you need it the most.

For example, imagine that there's only one car dealership in your town, and you need to buy a car. Think about how disappointed and dejected you would feel if your negotiations with the car dealer did not go at all the way you had hoped. The dealer would be well aware that his business was your only option, and he would take full advantage of the situation by making you agree to almost all of his concessions without having to agree to any of yours. Similarly, if you were the car dealer, what if the only customer who wanted to purchase a particular car decided to walk out the door? You'd either have to come up with even more concessions to try to get her to come back, or you'd just have to cut your losses.

In their renowned book *Getting to Yes* (1991), Roger Fisher and William Ury urge you to develop your **Best Alternative To a Negotiated Agreement** (BATNA) and follow it through so you always have something to measure against. If you plan to negotiate a raise from your boss, try to get another job offer before the discussion begins. This is your BATNA—your bargaining chip.

Plan B and Beyond

Whatever you're negotiating, you need to have at least one Plan B that's as lucrative as your original plan—or else you won't feel it's worth aspiring to when Plan A fails. Plan B should be carefully cultivated under the guise that it's actually an A-Plan. The same amount of research, prodding, and strategizing must be applied so you can spring right back into action if your original plan falls through. The more solid alternatives you have under your belt, the more poise you'll exhibit in front of the other party who—make no mistake about it—will probably sense the air of self-assurance that surrounds you.

Using Alternatives to Your Advantage

Unquestionably, the other party will have his own set of alternatives to bring to the table. Discovering what other options your negotiating adversary has lined up allows you to assess the level of confidence he has and to determine how much leverage the both of you have. If he doesn't have any options, or the ones you perceive he does have are weak, then you have the upper hand. Now, you may be tempted to have a lot of fun with this and get every little concession you can out of him. However, be mindful that some day the tables may be turned, and you'll be the one with no or few alternatives.

Once you've established your set of alternatives, use them throughout the negotiation to compare the options that are presented to you. If you're not sure about something the other party is offering you, ask yourself if you could get a better deal by utilizing one of your alternative plans.

One way to use your advantages for good is to use them as leverage. If at some point during the negotiation the other party has simply gone too far, mention that you have other options that you're prepared to use if things continue on an unsatisfactory level. One of two things will happen: She'll start meeting more of your demands, or she won't take you seriously, in which case you'll opt out of the negotiation altogether. Either way, you have the tools that allow you to move forward to accomplish the goals you've set out for yourself.

The Negotiation Meeting Schedule

Preparing an agenda for the meeting will help you stay focused, as well as help keep everyone else on track. The other party may also have a schedule to follow, in which case you'll have to compare both schedules to make sure everything gets covered. Be sure to make a copy of your schedule for each person attending the meeting so everyone knows ahead of time what will be scheduled (if it's a traditional business meeting; otherwise, a single copy for you will suffice). It's not necessary to schedule in breaks or lunches, since there's no telling when someone will need to take a breather.

You already know what goals you hope to achieve, how you plan on achieving them, and what concessions you're willing to make. Using this information to construct your schedule will help keep the meeting moving forward and may even serve as encouragement to seeing an end in sight!

In addition to keeping the meeting on track, schedules help remind everyone what has already been covered and what still needs to be addressed. There may be certain issues the other party hopes to avoid. Listing them on the schedule lets them know that those issues are important to you and will need to be discussed.

Putting Together a Schedule

The best way to create your schedule is to list all of the subjects that you want to cover. Assign each subject with a time frame that's appropriate to its level of importance and adhere to these time frames as closely as possible throughout the negotiation. Use your goals as a guide when determining which subjects require more time than others. Usually the touchiest subjects are slotted last on the docket since they'll most likely require long deliberations.

Without a Schedule

The schedule works as your backup, helping you to stay on track. Without a schedule in hand, your meeting can turn into chaos. Everyone will be thinking about a different issue, and no one will know when to transition from one to another. The velocity of the meeting may be too fast, causing some subjects to be overlooked and other subjects to be discussed too quickly. Allowing ample time for every subject is vital in making steps toward progress. Reserve large chunks of time for heartier matters that will be examined more carefully and in more detail. Trivial matters that need to be dealt with shouldn't use up a lot of your valuable time—they can be handled simply and efficiently.

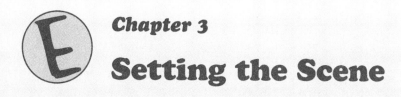

Chapter 3

Setting the Scene

The place where you choose to conduct negotiations is more important than you might have thought. Choose a location where you feel comfortable meeting the other party and discussing all the details, especially if they should be kept private. Consider the noise level and potential distraction. Don't forget that the space should be appropriate for the type of meeting you have in mind. You might want food served at the meeting or require access to the Internet or a slide projector.

Office Space

The office is the most traditional place to have a meeting and often the most comfortable. If you're meeting at your office, you have two basic options. If you have your own private office, you can use that (or ask a coworker to let you borrow his for the duration of the meeting); the other alternative is to reserve a conference room for the meeting.

FACT

Alliance Business Centers is a global company that rents completely serviced office spaces for very little money. They have a variety of locations all over the world and offer many more services, such as virtual offices and executive suites. Visit their Web site at *www.abcn.com* to learn more about their pricing.

Private Office

The private office should offer privacy and enough space for both parties. If you're having the meeting at your office, be sure to have your secretary hold all your calls, or if you don't have a secretary, turn the ringer off and voice mail on. You want as few distractions as possible—interruptions are discourteous toward the other party, particularly if she's traveled quite a distance to meet with you. You'll also want to make sure you have a generous amount of water or other beverages on hand, as well as extra pens, pencils, and paper. The other party will most likely come with everything she needs, but it's always a good idea to have the essentials on hand in case she's forgotten something.

Of course, there are a few drawbacks to conducting the meeting in a private office. Just because the door is closed doesn't mean people won't knock if they feel they have an emergency. One way to prevent intrusions is to notify everyone that you will be tied up in a meeting for a specified amount of time, and under no circumstances should you be interrupted.

Another drawback is that most offices are built with thin walls and doors (unless the host is a prestigious lawyer or CEO of a company). It's possible that a private room may not afford much privacy, and the meeting may be interrupted by conversations in the next room or across the hall.

The Conference Room

Conference rooms are usually built with thicker walls and doors and set away from heavily trafficked areas. The large space gives you and the other party more freedom to move around and stretch out, while the long table gives everyone all the room they need to spread out paperwork, keep notebooks and reference materials close by, and have refreshments and beverages at arm's reach.

If several people are attending the meeting, think about where you'd like each person to sit, placing people from the same party next to each other and leaders in seats where they can easily see everyone. If your conference room has large windows, make sure there are drapes available to be drawn. Extremely bright sunlight at the height of the day and noisy raindrops can cause distractions and even discomfort for some people.

Once everyone has arrived and seating has been discussed, point out the location of restrooms, water coolers, and break rooms for your guests. Now is also a good time to mention the company's smoking policy and point the way to any designated smoking areas.

The Home-Field Advantage

Ask anyone who's ever played a sport if their team was more likely to win a game when playing on their home turf, and you'll get a resounding "yes" almost every time. Reasons for this can be summed up in one word: home. When you think of your home, images of comfort, warmth, nostalgia, familiarity, love, friendship, and support are the first to enter into your mind. With all that positive energy on your side, it's no wonder your confidence level is up, your spirits are high, and your state of mind is bright.

Your Court

Playing on your turf has many advantages and very few disadvantages. When you're in your office, you have everything you need in proximity of where you're sitting. You know where all your important documents, notes, phone numbers, and contacts are, and you can easily find any piece of paper you randomly jotted bits of information on from your last phone call. You're in your space, surrounded by your stuff, backed by your people in your stomping grounds. You don't have to worry about whether you forgot to bring something to the meeting, and you get to comfortably sit in *your* chair behind *your* desk.

The major disadvantage to negotiating on your turf is that you can't just walk out if things are absolutely not going your way and there's no hope that they'll change any time soon. In that situation, the only thing left to do is stand up, make eye contact, hold out your hand, and thank the other party for coming by. If she seems surprised, explain that you'll need more time to think things through because none of your objectives are being met. At this point, she'll either ask you what needs to happen for the negotiation to continue, or she'll walk out the door and hopefully mull over what went wrong and contact you later on. Since you can't be the one to leave the room, creating an uncomfortable atmosphere for the other person is just as effective.

The Other Party's Court

There are some people who feel just as comfortable on the other party's turf as they do on their own. These sacred, magical beings are filled with confidence, make any office their office, and always come prepared.

If the other party requests to see a document that you don't feel comfortable showing, you can always say you didn't bring it with you and that you'll have to fax or e-mail it when you get back to your office. If someone's playing hardball or just isn't playing fair, you can allow yourself this one little victory and still respect yourself in the morning.

You too can follow in their divine footsteps by using the STOP technique (before you leave your office) each time you have to be the visiting team:

Shop your supply closet. Though the place you're going probably already has a roomful of office supplies, they won't have the specific things you like to have around. Your favorite pen, the calculator you feel most comfortable using, your company's letterhead, your business cards, highlighters, pocket dictionary, and anything else you keep handy in your own office should all be packed in your suitcase because they're all familiar items to you that make you feel more at ease and more at home while you're away.

Take everything with you. When in doubt, take it along. It's better to have too much of everything than not enough of the right thing. You never know what you might need, so here are few things that won't hurt you to take along: notes, forms, policies, price lists, rate information, discount procedures, basic contracts, print-outs of important e-mails, reference materials, names, phone numbers, addresses, and e-mail addresses of people you might need to contact, day planner, palm pilot, and so on.

Organize your briefcase. Keep important documents separate from miscellaneous documents, papers that are for your eyes only separate from those that you'll be sharing with the other party, and information not related to the meeting separate from information that is. Staying organized does wonders for the image you present to the other party. It makes you look professional, on the ball, intelligent, sincere, and ready for anything that comes your way. Besides, the more together you are, the more confident you'll feel, and the more capable you'll be at handling stressful situations when they arise.

Prepare for anything. Let's say one of your alternative negotiators has an office not too far from where you'll be negotiating with the current party. It's not a bad idea to prepare for a meeting with them in case things don't go well with this negotiation. You'll already have your materials by your side and you'll still be in the mindset to do business. And rather than risk forgetting something at your office a second time, you can continue to feel confident that you have everything you need.

Out At a Restaurant

While larger meetings are better kept inside the conference room, smaller meetings that include two to four people may be held at a restaurant. If you plan to combine negotiating with eating and think your meeting will be longer than two hours, check with the restaurant manager to see if it's okay to reserve a table for this long. Usually they won't mind, as long as you keep ordering items from the menu.

A restaurant is neutral territory that offers a relaxed atmosphere; people tend to feel more at ease around food. If your days are usually filled with staff or board meetings and you spend most of your time in your office, take the opportunity to get out of the building and try out a trendy new bistro or steakhouse. Chances are, the other party is used to spending her days confined to four walls too and will welcome the fresh scenery.

Keep Your Budget in Mind

There are a few things to consider when conducting your meeting at a restaurant. Since you may be there for a while, you don't want to choose a place that's too pricey, especially if you're not aware of the other party's financial situation. He may not have a corporate account to charge the meal. Though offering to pay for the entire meal is a nice gesture, it's not necessary and certainly not expected.

Avoid the Noise

Try to choose a restaurant that's not overcrowded or tightly packed in so you're not competing with the crowd to be heard. If possible, choose the most private area—usually in the corner in the back of the room, away from any television sets.

Whatever establishment you choose to dine in, don't sit next to the kitchen area, by the front door, or by the bathrooms. These high traffic areas produce a lot of hustle and bustle distractions, like clanging dishes and frequent loud calls of "Order's up!"

During the warmer months, you should take advantage of outdoor cafés that are tucked away in quaint parts of town. Surrounding yourself with nature's beauty will do wonders for your spirits and keep the meeting at a casual level of comfort. Coffee shops are also great meeting spots. You can spend hours there without ever being bothered.

ALERT!

Tempting as it may be, steer clear of downing too many alcoholic drinks. You want to stay focused and clear-headed, and you don't want to suddenly develop slurred speech, hiccups, or any other annoying condition related to having too much to drink. Keep it casual; there's no harm in having a glass of wine, but stop there.

At Home

Having a meeting at home is tricky—there are just too many distractions. If you have a home office, you may meet your clients there briefly, but hosting longer meetings at home isn't generally a good option. Still, if you plan to host the meeting at home, here are few tips that you can use to make the arrangement as professional and as effective as if you were at your work office.

Clean Up Your Act

Just like your personal appearance can make a positive or negative first impression, the state of your home will too. Be sure to clean your house thoroughly, and get rid of personal items and other clutter. And don't forget to turn off the television and the ringer on the main phone.

Pay special attention to your home office. Be sure there's a comfortable chair for your guest, and make a second one available for him to place his briefcase, jacket, and other items. You want to make the situation as comfortable as possible. You're perfectly at ease in your own office (and in your own home), so try to make the other party feel comfortable and "at home."

Kick Everybody Out

Your husband, wife, kids, and all pets should plan on staying out of the house for the duration of the meeting. Schedule your meeting to start in the morning while everyone's at work and school, and arrange to have a neighbor or a friend pet-sit for you. The house should be clear of all possible interruptions and distractions for as long as your guests are there. In fact, wait a few extra hours before you let everyone know it's okay to come back so you can take a nap, go for a swim, and have some time to yourself!

ALERT!

Remember, if the meeting is going poorly and you've just about had enough, you don't have the option to walk out of your own house. Moreover, you'll have to remain professional and find a polite way to ask the person you're dealing with to leave.

Over the Phone

What if you're not comfortable meeting with people face to face? There's nothing wrong with feeling more confident handling business matters via telephone. Do whatever works for you so you're able to perform your duties well. The only constraint is not using a cell phone. They are unstable, and it's easy to get a bad connection. You don't want to miss hearing any important details and end up agreeing to something you wouldn't normally agree to.

Even if you don't want to conduct all of your negotiations over the phone, you may need to rely on this form of communication once in a while. Sometimes it's simply more efficient, not to mention more cost effective, to do business over the phone rather than travel to meet the others in person.

Conference Calls

Negotiating is a game of details, and if you can't hear the details, you could end up taking some unnecessary losses and forfeiting a few gains. Keep this in mind when using the conference-call method for your next negotiation. True, it's convenient, but can everyone hear what the others are saying?

At the beginning of each call, introduce every person in the room to everyone on the other line, and identify who's in charge of the meeting if one person in particular has been assigned to the task. Discuss your agenda, time frames, and objectives, and ask the other party if they can hear you loud and clear. If you can't hear them, ask them to make adjustments until you can clearly hear every word.

The Right Equipment

Test the equipment you'll be using before the negotiation begins. Set up conferencing on the phone and ask coworkers to be on the other end so they can rate their level of clarity and you can rate yours. If there's any annoying buzzing, ringing, or static, find another phone or switch out the wires until the noise subsides. If it continues, plug the phone into another connection.

It's to your advantage to make the first call—you'll be at the top of your game and totally prepared. If the other party beats you to the punch and contacts you first, simply tell them you'll have to get back to them at a later date if you're not prepared.

Sometimes the equipment you or your company has is old and needs to be updated. There are many phones designed specifically for business purposes, such as conference calls and multiple-way calling, and some of them have better volume controls or other improved features. Check with your local Office Depot, Staples, or Radio Shack for all the latest models.

Relying on E-mail

At some point during the negotiation process, there's bound to be a paper trail of e-mail correspondences between you and the other party, you and your lawyer, and/or you and the contractor. Store all of these e-mails (including your responses) in a separate folder. It's also beneficial to print the e-mails and any attachments and keep them with all of your paperwork.

QUESTION?

What is "web conferencing"?
Web conferencing is when you use a particular company's services to host or participate in online meetings. Depending on the service and package you purchase, you can share PowerPoint slideshow presentations and other software that you have running on your machine. For instance, WebEx (at ✐*www.webex.com*) offers you a free, fourteen-day trial, and lets you view a Web seminar.

Regardless of how you organize your e-mails, you should have a backup system in place, especially if there's a substantial amount of material that reflects concessions that were made and rejected, agreements that were made, deadlines that have been set, prices, anything related to money, and important contact information. There are several ways you can back up your e-mails and attachments, and any other relative documents you've created:

- Save the information to a floppy disk.
- Using a CD burner, burn the information onto a writeable CD.
- Forward the information to a different e-mail address, one you can access from any computer.
- Immediately print a copy of e-mails that indicate any important decisions that have been made.
- Transfer the important information to a handheld organizer or similar device.
- Purchase a separate portable hard drive and back up the information there.

If you receive e-mails at both your home computer address and your work computer address, send everything to one central location, possibly a third address that you can access from any computer. This saves you from having to remember to forward work e-mails to your home address and vice versa.

Other Playgrounds

Some of the world's most important meetings are held on golf courses, in country clubs, at spas, and at other popular social gatherings. While you won't want the main part of your negotiations to take place at these sites, they make great meeting spots for when you and the other party just want to touch base and report progress.

Common interests are great things to share with your business partners. Not only does this important bonding experience show your human side and strengthen your relationship with your peers, but it also serves as a great resource for learning how to improve your swing. Remember that while business is after all just business, we're all still kids at heart, eager to be back in the sandbox to swap lunches and trade toys.

Chapter 4

Styles of Play

By now you should be feeling confident in your abilities to negotiate. You learned some ground rules for each step in the process, and you're ready to put all that research and planning to use. Not so fast! Before you jump right in, it's important to know how to recognize negotiating styles that attempt to derail your thinking to deter you from reaching your goals. Even more important, you need to know how to defend yourself against them.

The Intimidator

Intimidators employ tactics that aren't fair to most people because they prey on your emotions and prevent you from thinking clearly. They want you to feel like the negotiation is personal. They try to stop you from using your head by putting you on the defense in hopes that you'll use your bruised ego to stoop to their level of business. Is this starting to sound more like dealing with a psychological attack? That's exactly what it is. Intimidators take advantage of your human side, focusing less on the business aspect of what you're trying to accomplish and more on the individualistic side. They ambush you with negativity and sweep you up in a whirlwind of complete chaotic behavior that leaves you wondering what in the world just took place.

Intimidators know their methods are successful because when a person is worked up with feelings of anxiety, they'll usually do anything to stop feeling anxious and calm down. This is exactly what they are counting on. They want you to lose control and give into their demands just to be done with the stress of the deal. If you don't show these people that you won't tolerate their belligerent behavior, then you don't stand a chance.

Characteristics

If you're walking down the hall and hear someone shouting and slamming the phone down, you're listening to an intimidator in action. These people are loud, talk fast, make hurried movements, and sometimes use profanity to make a point. They interrupt constantly. Remember—they want to prevent you from thinking clearly so they try to distract you and cause you to lose your train of thought, especially when they don't like what they're hearing or they're not getting their way.

Intimidators will walk right into your office and start making demands, not suggestions or requests. Rather than accepting the workable solution that benefits the both of you, they'll tell you that they feel insulted by an offer of anything less than exactly what they wanted. They may start yelling again and even throw out a few expletives for extra drama.

Aside from pushing you around, intimidators try to frighten and annoy you by making threats. They might threaten to call off the entire negotiation or they might threaten to bring in someone from management. When intimidators use their supervisor as a threat, it is usually a bluff, in which case you should make it known that you welcome their superior's questions and concerns.

FACT

Car salespeople often create an intimidating image of their manager to prospective customers to try to scare them out of negotiating an automobile's price. These salespeople will tell the customer that they have to talk to their manager about the offer they made, only to return with a feigned look of anxiety or a negative response.

In contrast to the loud, antagonizing intimidators who try to bully others into a corner, there are those shrewd intimidators whose insolence is barely recognizable, yet penetrating once you pick up on it. Condescending by nature, these people know how to casually crawl under your skin and get on your last nerve with just a look, hand gesture, or blink of an eye. They don't intimidate you with scare tactics, they do it by acting as if they're far above you in every way, making you feel uncomfortable as they patronize both your person and your business sense.

Your Defense

The best way to defend yourself against intimidators is to avoid stooping to their level. Stay calm, focused, and in control. When the other person starts raising his voice, keep yours at an even tone. Displaying no emotion whatsoever shows them that you're not going to take the bait. You're a professional, and you're there to reach an agreement, not to get into a fight.

Another way to deter these people from emotionally breaking you down is to get the focus back on the issues at hand. Ask open-ended questions so that the other party doesn't try to brush you off with simple yes-and-no answers. Hopefully by forcing them to talk about the real reason you are both there, they'll cool down and realize you are not playing their game.

To handle the threat of completely pulling out of the negotiation, first find out if the intimidator is bluffing. If the threat appears to be legitimate, offer up a few of your concessions—but only if it means you'll be able to reach some of your own goals by doing so.

To stand up to belittling intimidators, use every bit of self-confidence you have. Without getting defensive or angry, continue to bring the focus back to the negotiation, and call them on their insinuations that they are better negotiators.

The Flatterer

The flatterer is similar to the intimidator in that she focuses more on your emotions than on what solutions you have to offer for reaching an agreement that you're both happy with. The difference is that this style of negotiating is loaded with insincere remarks that are meant to be personal and throw you off balance.

ALERT!

Flattery and intimidation can sometimes be used in conjunction as a different type of negotiating style, especially when related to gender. If a man and a woman are the two parties involved, the offending party might use gender-specific flattery ("You're an extremely beautiful woman" or "You look very handsome in that suit") as a way to intimidate the other person in an attempt to make him feel uncomfortable and lose his focus.

The flatterer knows that everyone loves to receive compliments, so she takes advantage of this by buttering up your ego. She may comment on your business style or flatter you with praise about your company, its products, and its CEO. Car salespeople will often tell you how good you look driving in one particular car and how great you could look driving home in another car.

You may be wondering about the point of all this ego-stroking. The flatterer makes you feel good by appealing to your emotional side in such a way that gives you a false sense of reality. For example, she'll try to make you believe that you have the upper hand and that you would be doing her a great favor by agreeing to certain concessions.

Undoubtedly you'd love to believe every good word that comes out of the flatterer's mouth, but you can't allow yourself to be manipulated. You should already think of yourself as a confident professional who is aware of her own strengths (and shortcomings), and you don't need to be reassured of these things during a business meeting.

You'll need to develop a thick skin for handling this type of player and learn to see through the sugary statements. These people are great at making promises but may not intend to live up to them. Go with what your instincts tell you. Seek advice from peers and supervisors, if needed, before you continue negotiations.

Characteristics

Since the flatterer tries to make the negotiation personal rather than professional, he may smile a lot and offer up many compliments right away. Throughout the negotiation, he might say something like this: "I know I can't pull one over on you, Bob, that's why I'm giving it to you straight right now." By presenting his offer to you in this way, he hopes you'll be so flattered that he recognizes your seasoned negotiating skills that you'll accept it and thank him for being honest with you.

Since extreme flattery is a form of dishonesty, it might be a good indicator as to whether the other party plans on fulfilling his side of the bargain. Try to recognize speech patterns and facial expressions when the flattering statement is made, and compare what you've noticed to that of the speech patterns and facial expressions that occur each time the other party agrees with one of your requests.

When the other party is intent on making you the main subject of the discussion, it's difficult to stay focused on the details about the issue you're talking about. It's also very easy to get sucked into all that wonderful praise because the other person is being pleasant and outgoing. However, you have to remember that you're there to create agreements that satisfy your business goals, not your personal goals.

Your Defense

The flatterer, like the intimidator, is an expert at tapping into your emotions, and you handle her the same way you handle the intimidator: redirect the focus back to the issues at hand. It's helpful to take notes because it keeps you on track, shows the other party that you mean business, and reinforces the fact that your goal is to achieve successful negotiations. Stay calm and don't let on that all the flattery is frustrating you. Shrug off the other party's remarks by asking open-ended questions that force her to talk about the details of the negotiation.

Another way to defend yourself against this kind of manipulation is to change your tone of voice to one of total indifference. Do not use inflections or interject any personality into your speech. By projecting a steely, emotionless image to the other party and refusing to react to all the sweet talk, she'll eventually come to realize that you're not succumbing to any of her tactics.

The Seducer

The seducer, as you can imagine, has a lot of charming tricks up his sleeve. He is the type of negotiator who paints a perfect picture for you and describes everything exactly as you want to hear it. But when it's time to get down to the nitty-gritty details, the illusion magically disappears. Suddenly, the ideal image you had in your head when you made your concessions has another side to it, one the seducer didn't show you until after he got you to agree with him.

Characteristics

The seducer is crafty and unethical and will make very attractive offers to you throughout the entire process of negotiating. Once he knows he's got you, he'll keep reeling you in little by little, telling you more of what you want to hear. As soon as you make the commitment, he fills you in on the fine print and swoops in with information like, "I agreed to that *before* you needed this." And just like that, the deal he's *really* offering you begins to emerge.

The seducer will often fail to live up to his part of the deal with reasons like "The paperwork is still being finalized," "My manager hasn't authorized it yet," or "I'm waiting to hear from my lawyer." These are clear indications that you're going to have to get your lawyer involved to get what's coming to you.

Your Defense

Protecting yourself from the seducer is simple: don't deal with him. This kind of manipulation, if not caught in time, can cost you in the long run. You might agree to things you thought were discussed in detail, only to find out later that there was a lot of fine print you didn't have the foresight to ask about. If it's too late and you already made agreements with this person, talk to a lawyer. If it's not too late and you've recognized the signs early on, simply leave the negotiation if you have other alternatives to consider.

One way to test the legitimacy of the seducer's promises is to ask a lot of questions. Asking a series of open-ended questions forces him to get back to reality and explain to you, in detail, what he's putting on the table. Find out exactly what it is he's offering you, and ask if his concessions are based on any contingencies.

If you decide to continue negotiating with the seducer, be sure you're informed about every detail of the agreements that are made. Ask questions, and lots of them. Be 100-percent sure you know exactly what's expected of you, and exactly what you're getting from the other person. Also, it's imperative that you take notes. Not only does note-taking help you remember everything that's said, it lets the seducer know you're paying attention to every word he utters and that you're on to his scheme.

The Complainer

Although the complainer is not as deceitful and unfair as the other negotiating personalities, you still need to be aware of the negative effects this type of person can have on your success. In fact, all the complainer really wants is to be heard and to be understood. Once she feels this has been accomplished, she becomes more reasonable and more pleasant to work with.

Characteristics

The complainer can sometimes come across as someone who employs the positional type of negotiating because she doesn't appear to be looking past her own needs. It might seem like she doesn't want to budge from her position, but in a way she's really looking for your help. She'll make statements such as, "How can you expect me to give you a free warranty when you're already asking me for a discount?" or "You have no idea how expensive it is for production to make the kinds of changes you're asking for." If you listen closely, there's a cry for help couched in those sentences.

When the complainer begins statements with "How can you" and "You have no idea," what she really wants is for you to ask her to explain what she means. For example, you would ask, "What is preventing you from giving me both a free warranty and a discount?" and "How expensive would it be for production to make these changes?" The complainer is filled with anxiety because she's dissatisfied with your requests and needs you to hear her out. She feels that you don't understand where she's coming from and why it's difficult for her to make the concessions you're asking of her.

Your Defense

You'll need a good ear and an empathetic heart to guard against the complainer. If you handle the situation with the right amount of patience and understanding, you could find yourself talking with a person who is not a positional negotiator at all.

As soon as the complainer starts voicing her concerns, let her have free reign of the airwaves. Hear every word she has to say, and encourage her to say more. Nod, make eye contact, and use hand gestures to let her know you are really listening to what she has to say. You could even plug in an "I see" or a "That's understandable" to verbally let her know you're acknowledging her and are actively listening. Your good ear is going to do wonders because once she's done letting it all out, you'll see the burden being lifted right off her shoulders as she begins to relax a little more.

Your job doesn't end at listening. Paraphrase a few of the complainer's key points to show that you empathize with her situation, and that you want to be sure you understand it correctly. Ask her to confirm what you've said; make the effort to understand where she's coming from.

Once you've finished listening to the complainer's point of view, ask more questions and slowly get back to the details of the negotiation. You might even offer a concession, a small one that you were saving for later, or one that you can afford to be a little flexible with. You need to show the complainer that you see her point and will try to make every effort to make the negotiation just as successful for her as you want it to be for yourself.

People will have a greater appreciation for you after you've listened to all their grumblings because you've given them the opportunity to get the issues out on the table to be dealt with head on. After you've allowed the complainer to say her piece, concessions can be made with a more comprehensive approach that satisfies both parties' objectives.

The Arguer

During the bargaining phase of the negotiation, your opponent may turn into an arguer. It's important to know that the arguer doesn't always start off arguing for its own sake, even though it may seem that way. Sometimes the main argument gets entwined with a bunch of little arguments and then every minor detail becomes an issue.

Characteristics

The arguer can easily be spotted if you pay attention to how often he debates your issues and requests. Let's face it: Bargaining is all about debating and arguing with the other side until you feel like you've won. However, you should learn the difference between what is worth arguing for and what isn't.

Here's a good rule of thumb. Ask yourself or the other party what the main concern for the argument is. Focus on resolving that issue first, but be aware of any meaningless arguments that pop up along the way. It's easy to get so caught up in trying to prove a point by using smaller, insignificant arguments to support your case that the real issue on hand is often lost along the way.

While debating the major issues between both parties is an expected part of the process, using empty arguments to stall the negotiation is not. When the arguer begins to challenge you with minor disagreements, he's most likely trying to throw you off track by pushing your buttons.

Your Defense

The arguer tends to pounce on your every move toward progress in order to stall the negotiation and buy more time for his case. Use the agenda you created and passed out before the meeting to remind him that you're on a schedule and you'd like to stick to it so that everything on the list is covered. Another line of defense is to ignore his aimless arguments by reacting to only the important ones.

FACT

Often what negotiators will do to handle this type of situation is take a break. Getting away from each other gives them room to clear their minds and re-energize. That way when they re-enter the room, they can start fresh and maybe even begin to resolve different issues instead of tackling the problem ones right away.

If the arguer still shows no sign of playing fair, tell him he's approaching your danger zone and that you're ready to walk out the door. Sometimes just getting your papers organized, gathering your belongings, and packing up your briefcase gets the message across.

The Logical Thinker

The logical thinker, reasonable though she may be, tends to overanalyze issues by lingering on them too long. She'll bring up valid points, which you might acknowledge but might not necessarily agree with. If you don't agree with them, she'll probe your reasons why until you've explained them thirty times, and then probe some more.

The logical thinker is extremely focused and insightful. She can support her beliefs with hard evidence and sound reasoning, which is why it's difficult for her to understand your reasons for disagreeing with her.

Characteristics

The logical thinker is a skeptic and is notorious for excessive questioning. However, his questions are not the frivolous "why" questions—they are specifically designed inquiries aimed at drawing conclusions, testing the validity of statements, weeding out inaccuracies, and evaluating information.

While it is quite impressive to watch the logical thinker in action, you don't want to fall prey to his tactics during a negotiation. Once caught in the web of questions he weaves around your arguments, it's difficult to break free.

Your Defense

The best defense you have against the logical thinker is to make every statement clear. Don't use convoluted language or statistics and facts you can't back up. Keep in mind that every person who asks a question isn't employing the logical thinker style of negotiating. It's when the questions keep coming, one after another, that you know you're dealing with a logical thinker.

Another way to repel the logical thinker's attack is to directly come out and ask, "What is it I can help you understand? What part of this doesn't make sense to you right now?" Keeping it simple and direct avoids the possibility of generating more questions.

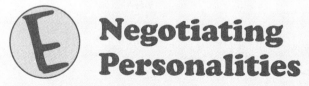

Chapter 5

Negotiating Personalities

People's negotiating styles are dependent on their personalities. Understanding your own personality and how it drives you will help you figure out your own negotiating style. It will also help you identify what kind of negotiator your counterpart is. Since part of successful negotiating involves knowing as much as you can about your counterpart, these clues are invaluable. They allow you to assess and predict the other party's behavior throughout the negotiation.

Aggressive and Dominating

You can identify an aggressive negotiator from the following personality traits:

- Demanding
- Pushy
- Bossy
- Self-centered
- Controlling
- Defensive
- Competitive
- Persistent
- Power junkie (enjoys power and respects people in power)
- Forceful
- Challenging
- Disdainful of weakness
- Rude
- Vengeful
- Easily angered
- Dominant
- Intimidating
- Ambitious
- Successful
- Impatient
- Shrewd
- Fast learning

These negotiators act fast and don't want to spend any more time with you than necessary. They usually are very busy, rarely with time for lunch, and they thrive in a fast-paced work environment. Before meeting with them, have all the facts prepared, and be ready for a speedy discussion. They have no patience and will try to rush you along every chance they get.

Handle these negotiators with care and know that they are always just seconds away from exploding into a fit of anger. They're not the type of people to hold back, and they're certainly not about to let you have any control over the discussion.

FACT

Aggressive personality types are said to have a "Type A" personality because of their high-speed way of life. They work constantly and are never satisfied with how much they're able to achieve. They also have a high risk for developing heart disease and are usually told to slow down by their doctors.

Their Objectives

Not only do these negotiators want to win at all costs, they want to win as much as they can and give as little as possible. Victory is their main goal, and they're used to getting their own way. They adopt a positional negotiating style, caring little for how you fare in the deal. Because they handle each encounter with a ruthless approach, they're easily riled up and tend to show no mercy.

Common Behaviors

During a negotiation, aggressive types make quick decisions and always try to get you to do the same. They never seem to have time for you, so they don't tolerate hesitation or thoughtful reflection. Threatening and personally attacking you seems perfectly normal to them because they believe that's how the game is played. If you're a sensitive person, do not negotiate with this personality or they will bring you to tears.

Their strategy involves withholding any information they think you might benefit from, inflating and deflating numbers, and embellishing or leaving out facts. They often throw temper tantrums and like to use the bottom-line technique because they always want to keep things moving quickly.

Passive and Submissive

This personality is the exact opposite of the aggressive personality. Submissive negotiators tend to exhibit the following characteristics:

- Nice
- Friendly
- Considerate
- Insecure
- Uncomfortable with conflict
- Fear not being liked
- Sensitive
- Shy
- Introverted
- Good listener
- Loner
- Calm
- Reserved
- Avoid being the center of attention
- Prefer to work alone or with few people rather than in groups
- Obedient
- Quiet

If you fall into this category, steer clear of holding any discussions with the aggressive negotiator. Because submissive personalities are more focused on pleasing other people, they get taken advantage of frequently.

If you are submissive and absolutely have to negotiate with an aggressive personality, you'll need to desensitize yourself before you begin. Resolve to be firm, focused, and determined to have your goals met.

Their Objectives

Submissive negotiators want others to like them. They'll do whatever they can to make the other party happy, even if it means giving up extra concessions or letting the other party renege on one of theirs. Because their main goal is to put the other party first, their secondary goals are usually focused on the other party's issues and how to satisfy them.

Common Behaviors

These people are the relationship-savers of a negotiation. They really can't bear the thought of someone being upset with them or showing disapproval of their actions. When this happens, they think they've hurt the other person's feelings and immediately begin working on solutions that mend the broken relationship.

Submissive personalities never take control of the negotiation. They don't like the limelight, and they're more comfortable following than leading. Consequently, they usually end up agreeing to everyone else's ideas, and they let the other party make all the decisions of the final agreement. They don't want to cause chaos or disturb the peace, so they rarely speak out of turn or voice their thoughts and opinions.

Logical and Analytical

Analytical people can be recognized by the following traits:

- Probing
- Apprehensive
- Mistrusting
- Fact-checker
- Thoughtful
- Organized
- Prepared
- Thinker
- Always early or on time
- Even-keeled

- Thrive on information
- Thorough with details
- Take time with decisions
- Sensitive
- Logical
- Fair
- Firm
- Critical

These negotiators need to have all the facts, details, and information to understand what's taking place at the negotiating table. Instead of rushing ahead, they want to be prepared first. They want to know what to expect before it happens so they can take the necessary steps to prepare for it.

Their Objectives

Analyzers like to problem-solve and seek deeper understanding of what they already know. Their main objective is to walk away from the negotiation feeling like they truly accomplished something. In order for them to achieve their goal, they must first be successful in reaching their secondary goals, which involves a careful review of all the available information, a logical approach to the solution, and an explanation of why it all works.

Common Behaviors

Expect people who have this personality type to walk into the meeting room with an armful of data. Also, rethink your strategy if it involves bluffing, stretching the truth, or skewing the facts—you can bet that somewhere in that stack of papers lies the truth. Another thing you can expect from them is a lot of questions. Though it may feel like you're on trial at first, it's important to know that this is how analyzers gather the information they need to make decisions. Be aware of how you answer them, too; they tend to be suspicious of a short, quick response, especially if it doesn't answer their question directly.

At some point during the discussion, you'll inevitably feel like you're under a microscope being closely examined and intensely scrutinized. That's because the other party is looking for errors in your argument, flaws with your concessions, and inconsistencies in your solutions. While this may come across as overcritical behavior, you have to remember that analyzers need to know that they've covered all bases before making a decision.

ALERT!

Analytical negotiators often take a long time to make decisions; they always feel like there's one more element they have yet to explore. Because of this, you'll need to give them a little push during closing or you'll be there for days waiting for them to approve the final agreement.

Whenever possible, have documentation to back up your justifications for certain concessions. Graphs, charts, slides, and reports are helpful too.

Friendly and Collaborative

The collaborative negotiator is easy to recognize from the following traits:

- Fair
- Courteous
- Empathetic
- Considerate
- Appreciative
- Understanding
- Honest
- Tactful
- Warm
- Friendly
- Successful
- Open-minded
- Resourceful
- Sincere
- Patient
- General concern for others
- Ability to employ creative-thinking techniques

- Flexible
- Sensitive
- Tolerant
- Great character and integrity

These are the ideal candidates for handling negotiations because they possess the principles needed to reach win/win solutions. They use all the steps outlined in this book to address the needs of all parties concerned. They understand that a negotiation is not a battle. Rather, it's a process of attaining mutual successes with the least possible amount of resistance and negativity.

Their Objectives

Collaborators are concerned with satisfying everyone's main goals by working toward results that allow them all to walk away from the table in agreement. It's also important to them to build trust and encourage and develop solid relationships that last well into the future. Their secondary goals include learning as much as possible about the other person and his objectives so that the desired outcome can be achieved.

QUESTION?

When you work with a collaborator, who directs the discussion and brings up new issues?
Once the discussion begins, ideas, thoughts, opinions, and concerns flow back and forth in a natural, easygoing current. The atmosphere is comfortable because collaborators have mastered the art of listening, and they invite you to share anything with them. You can expect this personality type to remain calm, professional, and active in searching for the best outcome.

Common Behaviors

Count your blessings if you're ever in the position of negotiating with a collaborator. You'll know right away by the warm smile, friendly handshake, and overall jovial carriage. At the same time, these negotiators display a keen business sense and make you feel like you're about to be part of something wonderful.

Evasive and Uncooperative

These negotiators can be recognized from the following traits:

- Insecure
- Fearful
- Careful
- Play it safe
- Don't like confrontation
- Introverted
- Timid
- Evasive
- Calm
- Reserved
- Procrastinator
- Nonresponsive
- Cold
- Pessimistic
- Easily embarrassed
- Indifferent

It's hard to imagine evasive negotiators at a negotiation because their way of dealing with issues is to disregard them altogether. That's not to say that they don't hope to succeed by walking away with all their needs met; they just doesn't know how to approach the issues, so they don't approach them at all. Evasive negotiators usually oscillate between what to do and what not to do because they're so afraid of making the wrong move and being crushed by the opposing party.

Their Objectives

One of the major goals of these negotiators is to endure the negotiation and to try not to lose. The reason for this struggle could be insecurity, lack of knowledge about the subject, or anything else that may make them feel too uncomfortable to participate. Throughout it all, their only survival technique is to avoid saying anything that might cause a disagreement or further discussion of the issues.

Common Behaviors

It's easy to get frustrated with this negotiating type because they're always postponing the discussion of subjects that might cause a debate. As a result of putting everything off, a lot of unresolved issues arise, and the feeling of getting nothing accomplished takes over. In addition, communication begins to break down because of their further avoidance of those same issues when they resurface later. It's a difficult cycle to break once it begins because the nature of this type of personality is to avoid tension, confrontation, aggressiveness, anger, and any problem that comes about.

Expressive and Communicative

Expressive negotiators may be any of the following:

- Playful
- Spontaneous
- Energetic
- Talkative
- Sociable
- Self-involved
- A "people person"
- Open
- Easily distracted
- Short attention span
- Enthusiastic
- Think out loud
- Extrovert
- Like being the center of attention
- Ambitious
- Not a good listener
- Like to be reassured

These negotiators are generally very animated and always portray a fun-loving attitude in any situation. It's important to build rapport with them at the beginning of the negotiation because it makes them more comfortable when they know people are enjoying their company. It also allows them to work their "magic" on you by completely winning you over with their charm.

Their Objectives

Aside from becoming your new best friend, the main goal of expressive negotiators is to see how much they can get out of the deal by using their social skills and optimism. When you reject one of their offers, they tend to take it personally. They fail to understand how the discussion could be about anything other than them. They spent a lot of time hamming it up with you, and they expect to be rewarded!

Common Behaviors

There's no denying that expressive negotiators have an upbeat personality that's like a breath of fresh air in the conference room. Instead of conducting business in a stuffy, even-mannered tone, they try to have as much fun as they would if they were at one of their social functions. However, you need to constantly redirect their focus back to the issues under discussion because they're quick to jump from one subject to the next without resolving anything first. In an excitable rush to get their thoughts out in the open, they take advantage of every gap in the conversation to voice their needs. If you don't take the opportunity when it comes your way, you might never get a word in.

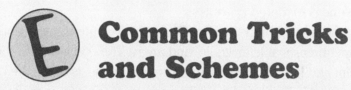

Chapter 6

Common Tricks and Schemes

Sly negotiators often rely on techniques designed to manipulate and deceive their opponents by toying with their emotions. While it's not advisable to use all of the ploys described in this chapter to achieve win/win success, knowing how to recognize them is your best defense against falling for these tricks. This chapter explores some of the most common tactics used during negotiations.

Good Guy/Bad Guy

Probably the most easily recognizable trick is the good guy/bad guy tactic, an entertaining display of two people who are on the same team but act out completely opposite roles in an effort to control your emotions with their distortion of reality. If the good guy/bad guy act is successful, the victim of this mind game is rendered powerless.

Here's how the technique works. The bad guy is the disagreeable negotiator, always unreasonable, irritable, and angry. The good guy, on the other hand, is calm and helpful, the peacemaker who interjects to tell the bad guy to ease up a little bit. This good guy/bad guy routine is set up to make you feel like the good guy is on your side and will do whatever he can to help you.

Surely you've viewed this scene on a television show or in a movie. The bad cop interrogates the murder suspect by screaming, threatening, and bullying him, then storms out of the interrogation room only to be replaced by the good cop who befriends the suspect by offering him cigarettes, being nice to him, and promising to help him out of the situation he's in if he just reveals where the murder weapon is or where the body is buried.

Another place you might have witnessed this scenario is at the car dealership. The salesperson will play the good guy and his manager, who is never seen, plays the bad guy who won't let the salesperson make any concessions to you. The salesperson will go back and forth to his manager's office and always come back saying he did everything he could to get what you wanted, but the manager refuses to budge.

ALERT!

As you can see, this tag-team approach is a combination of the intimidator and seducer working together to take control of the other person's mental state. While one causes fear, anxiety, and stress, the other serves to relieve the person of his worries by using false hopes and attractive offers to reassure him.

When you encounter this duo during negotiations, the bad guy will attempt to intimidate you and is sure to reject every offer you make—he may even rush out of the room in a huff. Then, the good guy will come in to the rescue and will let you know he's on your side. Because this technique is not difficult to identify, you'll be able to counter it right away. There are several ways you can do this:

- Tell them that from here on out you want to negotiate with the good guy only. By eliminating the bad guy, the plan becomes useless.
- Call them on it. Ask them how long they plan on playing the good guy/bad guy performance for you. They'll get embarrassed, and the bad guy will suddenly disappear.
- Play along. Pretend to be alarmed by their statements, then call off the negotiation all together. As soon as you begin packing your brief-case, they'll be asking you to come back to work it out.
- Develop your own bad guy. Tell them you'd be more than happy to agree to their demands, but you have a supervisor who never bends the rules. You can get creative with how rough and tough you make your bad guy out to be.
- Tell the good guy you'd like to speak to him privately. Once alone, tell him you're about to walk away from this negotiation because of the bad guy's behavior and lack of professionalism. Tell him you're taking a five-minute break and expect that he will talk with his partner and advise him to back off.

Remember to employ one of these counters as soon as you know you're being duped. Getting the bad guy out of the picture early in the game allows the rest of the negotiation to progress. However, you'll have to keep a sharp eye out for any other techniques the other party might try to use on you.

Shills and Decoys

Shills are basically sales pitches or people who act as bait to lure customers; decoys are what you use to divert attention away from the real issues. Shills are often used in casinos, where managers will have casino employees posing as customers stationed at slot machines, winning jackpot after jackpot, or at blackjack tables, having fun and showing their excitement with whoops, clapping, and laughter. The logic is that customers will be attracted to the machines that seem to be "hot" and drawn to the blackjack tables, where people seem to be having a great time.

People use decoys all the time, usually to get a reduction in price for something. For example, let's say you're at a restaurant and the waitress brings you the wrong order. You send it back and patiently wait for the dinner you wanted. Meanwhile, your friend is eating her meal and will be almost finished by the time your food arrives. If you feel you should get a discount on the bill, you'll explain to the waitress how you and your friend couldn't have the luxury of eating your meals together because of the inconvenient mix-up, and proceed to ask for the bill to be reduced to make up for your troubles.

The decoy in this example is the fact that the order was taken wrong and you had to wait even longer for your meal. Even though you understand that mistakes happen and would be willing to pay full price, the issue is that you want to see if you can get a discount. By using a decoy to take the focus off wanting to get a discount, you're able to use the waitress's mistake to your advantage.

Some decoys are set up deliberately. A contractor, for example, might intentionally come up with a small estimation error in your favor and use it as leverage against you. When you point the error out to him, he'll tell you he'll concede to it but only in exchange for something else from you. In this case, you will be tricked into giving him a concession you normally wouldn't have because the estimate was actually not in error.

During the bargaining part of the negotiation, the other party might try to use a decoy against you. If this happens, keep the focus on the issue. For instance, if the other party is persistent in trying to get you to reduce production fees, ask questions that are aimed at determining the real problem.

The Straw-Man Technique

Straw-man techniques involve making the other party believe something is valuable to you when it really isn't. Each concession made during the negotiations is made to seem like the negotiator is giving up a lot, even if that's not actually the case. Negotiators who rely on the straw-man technique never let on that the concession they are making isn't that big of a deal.

Let's say that during the negotiation process of selling your house the buyers want you to include the washing and drying machine in the sale. Since you already planned on buying a new set for your new house, leaving the old washer and dryer at the house was something you already considered doing. But instead of telling the buyer that, you display an attitude of concern and contemplation. Let them think this is a tough decision for you to make so you can use this concession in exchange for one of theirs. You can say you'll include the washer and dryer if they take responsibility for getting the broken tiles in the bathroom fixed.

QUESTION?

What is bundling?
Bundling is a clever way of getting the other party to make two or more concessions at once by clustering them together so they seem contingent upon each other. For example, when the other party is fully committed to all the agreements that have been made, and all the papers have been signed, you ask them to pay for certain fees. They'll usually agree since everything has been settled already.

Another example of the straw-man tactic is using an unnecessary delay to trade for something else of value. For example, the other party will tell you that they need more time to sleep on an issue, but then offer to give you a decision right away—in exchange for a concession. When you hear that offer, you'll know that they really don't need to take the extra time to make up their minds. What they're doing is using the straw-man technique.

One way to counter the straw-man tactic is to let the other party make all the offers first. This allows you to ask questions that reveal their needs and concerns, and leaves you in a position to use the straw-man tactic on them. Another method is to make them feel guilty for bluffing by commenting on how you're looking forward to building a positive relationship with their company and anticipate being part of the growth that your company and theirs will be sharing. Also let them know that there are great opportunities for both companies to work together again in the future. After hearing these statements, the other party will be less likely to use the straw-man tactic because he doesn't want to risk jeopardizing the trust you share and therefore also jeopardizing the possibility of more business.

Taken by Surprise

In yet another attempt to throw you off guard, the other party plans what seems to you like a totally unexpected twist in the negotiation. In an instant, he brings up new information or displays a new behavior that he hopes will generate an emotional reaction from you. The reason for this is threefold.

First, he wants to break your concentration and take you away from focusing on your objectives and achieving your goals. By suddenly erupting into a fit of anger, for example, he intends to stir up your emotions and hopes that you respond with fear, shock, or frustration. If you take the bait and respond with an equal amount of anger, it may be a while before you get back to discussing the issues at hand.

Second, he anticipates your negotiation efforts to be thrown off-kilter once you let your guard down and give him an emotional response. If, for example, you react with anger, you may say something that he can use against you later when he's trying to deflate your character or prove one of his points.

Lastly, he tries to get an emotional outburst from you because he's hoping for the possibility that you'll concede something you previously did not want to concede. For example, if you react with shock or fear, you might be more likely to agree with him on an issue you were struggling with earlier.

Luckily, there are several ways to counter this assault on your emotional well being:

- **Do not react.** Since that's exactly what the other party is hoping for, simply do not give in to his ploys. Stay calm and show your professionalism.
- **Take a break.** Give yourself time to let the new information sink in or to cool off.
- **Ask for details.** Learn as much as you can about the new information you've just been given, and determine if it's truly something to be worried about.
- **Call for help.** If the other party introduces new information to the negotiation and you're not prepared to handle it, get together with your team to discuss how to handle the new information.

Some negotiators are known for using surprise tactics. If you know that you're dealing with such a negotiator ahead of time, mentally prepare yourself for it by making a list of statements you can deliver that will redirect the focus back to the negotiation. This will help you remain unaffected by the other party's attempts to disrupt your composure.

Sometimes the surprise can be that a party member, usually a supervisor, is unable to attend one of the meetings so he sends another person to take his place. This person then tries to tire you out by asking you to bring him up to speed on the negotiation and to answer all his questions about why you're not being flexible on a particular issue. By prodding you for the same information over and over again, he's hoping you get so drained by the process that you'll just give into his concessions without putting up another fight.

Add-ons and Nibbling

These two tactics are a bigger deal than their names suggest. When used in negotiations, they're made to sound like small requests that don't deserve the attention larger issues usually require. If you're not careful, this misconception can cause you to give away a lot more than you think.

An add-on is a small concession that a negotiator asks for and adds to the end of a larger concession that's already being discussed. For example, "I'll buy your product if you throw in a free one-year warranty." If you never intended to give the free warranty, do not feel pressured to do so now. Similarly, do not feel like you were "taken" if you do decide to agree to the concession; make sure it's something you feel comfortable with before giving in to the other party.

"Nibbling" is a term used to describe the manner in which a negotiator will ask for "one last thing" after you've already reached a mutually beneficial agreement. These kinds of people are rarely ever satisfied with the agreements that have been made, and they always need to ask for another concession, and another, and another. He'll usually use excuses like, he "forgot to ask before" or "something has suddenly come up" and he needs to make a change or two.

The only way to stop these tactics in their tracks is to confront them head on. If you notice that the negotiator is continuously asking for extras, especially after everything has been finalized, simply ask her if she's happy with the deal the way it is. If she says yes, then tell her you feel that a fair settlement has been made and you see no reason to make any more changes. Usually she'll back down at this point because she feels like she gave it her best shot and can live without the concession. If she doesn't back down, ask her if you can make some changes as well.

ALERT!

Just because it *sounds* like the negotiator is asking for a small concession doesn't mean the concession is small. Before agreeing to his request, determine if doing so will help you achieve your goals and objectives.

Additional Techniques

Among the many negotiating tricks and ploys that you will encounter, here are some of the more commonly used ones that you should definitely watch out for:

Funny money. This is real money that you tend to think of as not being real. When gambling, you exchange hundred-dollar bills for chips, a tactic casinos employ to make customers feel like they're not spending "real" money, when in fact that's exactly what they're doing. In negotiating, the other party might use funny money to shift your focus away from cost or price. For example, instead of talking about dollar amounts, they may discuss percentages or points.

Red herring. A person makes a fake demand, only to trade it off later for another one. For example, if the real issue at hand is to get you to agree to a 20-percent discount on production fees, the other party might start off with demanding something higher, like a free three-year service warranty. When you decline the warranty offer, the negotiator will then say she will trade the warranty request for the 20-percent discount.

Lowballing. This tactic is used primarily in the retail industry. When comparison-shopping for a computer, for example, one retailer might tell you he can sell it to you for under a specified dollar amount—much lower than the competitors' prices. After researching several stores and discovering that all of their prices were significantly higher than what the first retailer offered, you return to the first store only to find that you're being refused the price you were told you could get. Excuses you can expect to hear are as follows: The salesperson's manager won't approve the price, the price was a one-time offer, the figure was miscalculated, or the salesperson who gave you the quote is not working on the day you go into the store.

Flinching. Let's say the other party threw a dollar amount out there, but didn't really expect you to go along with it. Why would he suggest it if he didn't think you'd agree to it? Because he wants to see what kind of visual reaction you give him. If you have no reaction whatsoever, he might assume that getting the amount is a possibility. However, if you gasped in shock or put your hands on your cheeks and dropped your jaw, he'll drop his price because it's obvious you're not happy with the price he gave you. When the other party gives you an outrageous dollar amount, don't hold your feelings back. Instead, use flinching to convey how much you disagree. Don't forget—flinching is also effective on the telephone.

Crunch. The negotiator uses this tactic to make you doubt your position by disagreeing with everything you offer, using terms like, "You'll have to do much better than that" and "That's just not good enough for me." The negotiator who uses this method is never satisfied and often makes you feel lucky to get another chance at making a different offer. Since she'll never give you reasons why your offers are not good enough, you'll need to ask her for details about why they seem so unreasonable to her.

Escalation. When you have enough leverage to get more out of a deal than what has already been agreed upon, you're employing the escalation tactic. You get away with it usually because the other party is already so emotionally involved that he doesn't want to back out of the deal.

Bogey. The bogey is essentially used as a scapegoat when trying to explain the inflexibility of the other party. For example, the negotiator will blame a third party, for example her manager, for why she cannot come down in the cost of production fees. When you detect a bogey, ask to speak to the person in charge of creating the bogey and continue negotiating with her instead. Remember, you want to negotiate with the person who has the authority to make and accept concessions.

As you learn about these negotiating techniques, keep in mind that some are not as ethical as others. Even if you choose not to use them, it's a good idea to learn how to recognize them in your opponents.

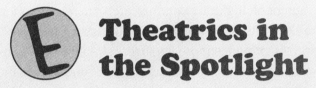

Chapter 7

Theatrics in the Spotlight

When you're at the negotiating table, the last person you hope to meet is a full-time actor—someone who's mastered bluffing and other tactics and tricks, using them without being noticed. This chapter rolls out the red carpet and shines the spotlight on which actors you can expect to make an appearance—and what you can learn from their behavior.

Playing Dumb

Some negotiators pretend to be unprepared or uninformed about the subject under discussion. Playing dumb and asking lots of questions may help you acquire a lot of information from the other party. When used properly, the tactic becomes a valuable learning tool that can uncover information pertinent to your argument. If, during your research, there were a few questions you were unable to answer, skirting around the issue by asking indirect questions can help you formulate more intelligent strategies. Instead of risking uncomfortable confrontation by coming right out and asking the question, "Why did your production department fail to meet its yearly quota?" it might be more suitable to ask what the production department's numbers were for the year and how they compared to previous years. The other party will be less defensive about the subject and more willing to explain the decline in numbers.

Another favorable outcome of this tactic is that it allows you to confirm information you already know. Further, it makes the other person aware that you're privy to his information. If you're taking your car to a certain mechanic for the first time, you can ask a few questions to let the person know you've done your research and are not the kind of person he can take advantage of:

- Does the shop have a AAA rating?
- Is it ASE (Automotive Service Excellence) certified?
- Is every mechanic working in the shop certified?
- Where are parts purchased?

If the person you're negotiating with starts to play dumb, don't allow the main issue to be derailed by peripheral information that the other party intends to use against you. Ask him right away if there's a deeper issue he would like to talk about, and try to determine where his questions are going. It may simply be that he needs the information and doesn't have it on hand. Just be aware of incessant digging and suspend it before the discussion plays out more like a trial.

When your counterpart uses the "just play dumb" tactic, you can be certain he's searching for something that will strengthen his confidence in presenting or rebutting a concession or important issue. For example, he might have sensed early on in the discussion that you were bluffing about something. In order to get you to reveal what you're hiding, he'll pretend to be ignorant and ask all sorts of questions that relate to his suspicions. This in turn helps him draw conclusions about what he thinks you're holding back. It also gives him something to refer to when he eventually confronts you with his skepticism.

The Socratic Method

One way to tell if the other party is playing dumb is to recognize the signs of the Socratic method, a technique of asking leading questions in order to manipulate the other person into giving a particular response. No matter how many questions you answer, more will follow, until you give an answer the other party finds satisfactory.

FACT

The Greek philosopher Socrates taught his students how to logically think about and argue the statements they made by engaging them in a philosophical debate, ultimately concluding in a contradiction of the original statement. By actively participating in the debate, the students learned to think for themselves and could see through the trap of Socrates' questioning.

You can avoid this power tactic by redirecting every question to a main objective, asking how the question pertains to the goals you are both trying to reach. Explain that you don't want to waste time on trivial inquiries that don't lead to solutions. If there are some questions that your counterpart insists on asking, keep your answers short to deflect further questioning.

Diffusing a Tense Situation

Resist the urge to try the Socratic method on your negotiating counterpart; your attempt at manipulation may backfire. However, it is a good idea to play dumb when the other party's behavior becomes antagonistic. If his competitive spirit is getting the best of him, not to mention getting in the way of progress, a little ego stroking will have a calming effect and allow the discussion to continue in a professional manner. To produce this effect, pretend you don't know much about a particular issue your counterpart wants to discuss, and ask for information about it using open-ended questions. He'll be more than happy to assist you because he'll view your lack of knowledge as a sign of weakness.

ALERT!

People who operate from ego alone often confuse confidence with a know-it-all attitude. Worse, they then get defensive and try to assert themselves because they feel threatened by the person exuding the confident behavior. If this bomb isn't defused early, unnecessary conflicts could arise.

Conducting Interrogations

When a negotiator relies on questioning, it's important to try and figure out what kind of information he is really looking for. Questions serve many functions, and not all of them conceal a hidden agenda. Nevertheless, it pays to be on your guard. Conversely, if you're the one asking questions, consider formulating them in such a way as to get better responses. By learning to recognize various question types, you will be able to put together questions that are skillfully thought out and suitably targeted.

Vague Questions

Asking vague questions can prompt an unexpected response because these questions don't lead to a specific answer. If the other party asks vague questions, it's easy to misinterpret what they really mean, and you might give an answer that you did not intend to disclose. For example, when answering the question, "That figure isn't accurate, is it?" you might inadvertently reveal that the number is adjustable when you weren't ready to discuss that point yet. To avoid this, ask the other party to elaborate on his question by being more specific: "Why don't you agree with the figure? Is it too high or too low?" If your counterpart is just digging around for information, get exact details about what he wants to know before you give too much away.

Loaded Questions

When you stop to examine a loaded question, you will find that it is actually more like a judgment wrapped up in a pretty little package topped off with a carefully tied question mark. It sounds like you are being asked a question, but you are really being slighted by the remark contained within the query. Usually, the presumption is a negative one, such as in the questions, "Is your staff still unorganized?" and "Is your unfair request still on the table?" The way to deflect these attacks is to, once again, ask for clarification before answering.

If you answer right away, you validate the other person's opinion that your staff *is* unorganized and your request *is* unfair. Defend yourself by asking him why he thinks your staff is disorderly and why your request seems unreasonable to him.

Leading Questions

Lawyers use these questions frequently, and when they do, an objection from the opposing lawyer is not slow to follow. A leading question is the kind of question that tries to get a specific response, usually to prove the asker's point.

In the courtroom, a leading question is often used to create a dramatic presentation for the jury. The opposing lawyer objects to a leading question because the questioning is usually irrelevant to the trial and serves only to trick the witness into saying something out of context. Further, the process is unfair to the witness. The lawyer already knows the answers to the questions he is asking; he knows the script and is acting it out using the witness as his unknowing sidekick.

Many questions arise during negotiations, but if you think the other party is using leading questions to prove a point, kindly remind her that you are not on trial and that you would like to save time by discussing only the heart of the issues.

Talking, Talking, and More Talking

A well-balanced discussion involves an equal amount of talking and listening among all parties. All negotiators want to feel that what they're saying is important to the rest of the table. When given the chance, however, some people dominate the conversation or discussion by talking entirely too much. Sometimes this is done intentionally, and sometimes the person doesn't even realize how much he's talking. Either way, excessive talking during a negotiation can throw you off-center. By the time the other person finishes speaking, you might have forgotten thoughts you had about certain points that were brought up earlier in the discussion.

If you realize that you've been chattering nonstop, stop talking right then and there. Apologize for controlling the conversation, and give the other party the floor. Acknowledging your mistake (instead of covering it up) will help you regain the respect you might have lost.

A verbal takeover is never a good idea. It makes the other party feel as though his objectives are of no concern to you. As a result, you can lose his attention as well as his desire to share information with you.

Reasons for Rambling

The more aware you become of your counterpart's negotiating style, the more you'll be able to correctly guess what his intentions are and why he behaves in certain ways. As mentioned previously, a rant can be either deliberate or purely accidental. Before you react, use the following guide to determine which behavior is being displayed.

Deliberate

- ☐ Does not give you the opportunity to interject with comments or questions, even when you signal that you have something to add.
- ☐ Shrugs off your comments and questions, or says, "Let's talk about that later."
- ☐ Interrupts you whenever it is your turn to speak.

Accidental

- ☐ Repeats thoughts, speaks quickly, and uses a lot of run-on sentences; this could be a sign of nervousness and insecurity.
- ☐ Makes a lot of jokes and aimless chitchat; although it may seem this person is avoiding the issues, these could be signs of an attempt to make a good impression.
- ☐ Fills silences by talking about more concerns or goals; this person may be uncomfortable with long periods of silence or could be thinking out loud.

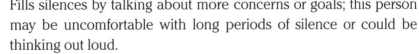

Some people use talking as a way to compensate for what they lack in leverage or offers. The less they have going for them, the more they feel the need to talk in order to make it appear that the opposite is true.

Information Overload

Excessive talking can be used as a tactic in an effort to bombard you with so much information that you miss all the important points. First, the other party gives you all the pertinent facts up front, and then he delivers a deluge of information that has you trying to focus on too many points. Finally, he concludes with details that are even further from the issues and facts already discussed. The purpose of this ploy is to overwhelm you with so much data that you forget the questions you had about the real issues, fail to notice erroneous assumptions, and miss the chance to inquire about gray areas.

It can be difficult to get a straight answer from people who tend to ramble. The longer the answer, the harder it becomes to extract the information you need. If necessary, ask the question again and again until you are clear about the real answer. If the other person tries to evade the question by using doublespeak, keep pressing. If you want to know how much her company charges in production fees, don't let her get away with an answer like, "Well, it's usually 10 percent, but it has been 20 percent in the past." As you can see, the question still remains to be answered.

FACT

When a person speaks for sixty minutes, we tend to remember only what was said during the last five minutes. The same holds true for someone who speaks for forty-five, thirty, or twenty minutes. Take notes every time you and your counterpart confer to make sure you remember everything that's being said.

A Shouting Match

Most people feel uneasy when someone is yelling at them, and they are embarrassed when people can hear it, even if they didn't do anything wrong. Shouters know this. They use that discomfort to their advantage by creating melodramatic scenes. They have no shame and will resort to this tactic to get their own way.

Not everyone shouts for the same reason, so listen carefully to pick up on the cues. She might be shouting because she feels threatened or intimidated by your expertise. In this case, you can put her at ease by asking for her advice on a particular issue or by asking her to explain a few things to you. This will give her the self-confidence to carry on the conversation with professionalism rather than from a defensive attitude.

Another reason that the other party might resort to shouting is because he is under a lot of pressure from his superiors. He is expected to walk away from the deal with specific concessions or to adhere to a strict deadline. Restore his confidence in your desire to produce a win/win outcome by showing empathy.

ALERT!

The worst thing you can do when your counterpart starts shouting at you is to shout back. Doing so gives him all the more reason to continue shouting. Instead, calmly tell him to back off, and then shift the focus back to a factual debate. Your composure will stop him from yelling and calm him down.

Emotional Outbursts

Negotiators who have learned to become seasoned actors know just when to use their skills to get what they want. In addition to shouting, they might stage tears, put on an air of unconcern, or try to scare you with threats. Whichever character they get into, their purpose is to tap into your emotions and control the way you think. It's also a way for them to see how malleable you are. Can you be easily swayed? Or are you focused?

If the other party can create self-doubt in your mind, then she knows she can also get you to rethink your position. When you encounter these theatrics, ignore them. Announce that you would like to take a break to give the other party some time to compose herself. You can also offer to postpone the negotiation. This will usually get the message across that you have no intention of giving in to any kind of theatrical performances.

What kind of emotional outbursts can I expect?
An explosion of anger is the commonest kind of outburst. Sob stories and guilt trips are frequently used to make you believe that the situation is worse than it is. Helplessness creates an uncomfortable situation because the other party wants you to think that he's giving up, and there's only one thing you can do to get him to come back. If you give into this act, he'll only use it again.

Blatant Mistreatment

Abuse comes in many varieties—none of which should ever be tolerated. The intention of the abuser is to wreak havoc on your ego in order to achieve his own goals. Abusers use personal attacks to insult your intelligence. Verbal abuse—in the form of name-calling, foul language, emotional exploitation, manipulation, and cruelty—is intended to shake your self-confidence and well-being.

If you feel you're a victim of abuse, let the other party know that you will not accept that kind of behavior and then walk out. If you don't defend yourself, he will lose respect for you and continue acting offensively toward you.

If you are ever physically abused during a negotiation, don't perpetuate the violence by fighting back. Instead, walk out and don't look back. If the other party calls to apologize, accept the apology, but don't agree to meet with him again. Tell him you would prefer to work with his supervisor or another employee of the company. And just in case his coworker uses the same technique, bring a lawyer to the meeting.

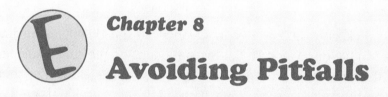

Chapter 8

Avoiding Pitfalls

Negotiating for the first time can be intimidating, and you are bound to make a few mistakes along the way. That's okay; it's part of the learning process. Even the most experienced negotiators think about how they could have done things differently. Like chess, negotiating involves learning the rules, studying different players' styles, and developing your own skill over time. To help you in your learning process, here are some pitfalls you'd do well to avoid.

Dealing with Difficult People

Everyone has a different outlook on life. Our individual experiences influence how we see the rest of world and how we react to what we encounter. When two or more parties sit down at the negotiating table, each person has a different perspective on the situation and operates directly from that viewpoint.

The trick is to find a way to balance all the different personalities involved in the discussion so the focus remains on the subject matter and not on the individuals themselves. Meeting this challenge can be mentally exhausting and physically tiresome if one of the personalities is uncooperative by nature or if it clashes with your own.

When the person becomes the problem, the deal-making process can be grueling and unpleasant to endure. It's hard to concentrate on your strategy when you feel like you're walking on eggshells, worrying about how the other person will respond to your next statement or feeling frustrated because you can't find a way to get along. Deal with this problem early on by acknowledging that you do in fact have a common interest—the objectives that brought you both to the table in the first place.

Reaching an Understanding

If the other party refuses to be accommodating, fights you every step of the way, and continues to use positional negotiating, examine the behavior by openly discussing it. Let her know how you view the situation, and talk about how your personality differences prevent the two of you from working toward a win/win outcome. For example, you might be frustrated with her quick, defensive reactions to your requests, while she might be impatient with your slow responses. By calling attention to these differences, you might discover that she's used to working in a fast-paced environment and handling every situation with speed. She in turn could benefit from learning that your slower approach isn't deliberate; you have a tendency to analyze everything.

Try to understand where the other party is coming from, and be open about where you stand. Don't place blame or get upset because she'll be less likely to work out the problem with you.

If the other party continues to be difficult, illustrate how you have put your differences aside to create a more comfortable atmosphere. Ask that she afford you the same courtesy. Let her know that while you respect her opinions, you'd like to focus on solutions that make the deal work, not the actions that destroy its progress.

Choose Words Carefully

The English language contains a few seemingly innocent words that can surprise you with how much power they truly hold. Tucked inside a harmless sentence, these words can create a tone that sounds offensive to anyone who already has a defensive personality. Although your intention is not to be hurtful, the other party misunderstands your statement and reacts negatively to it.

Fine-tune your speech to avoid unknowingly sounding aggressive by making the following adjustments to your word choices:

"I" vs. "you"—Instead of saying, "You still didn't answer my question," rephrase the statement: "I'm sorry, I still don't understand. I think a few examples can give me a better idea." By placing the blame on yourself, the other party doesn't feel like you're criticizing and is more willing to communicate.

Negative vs. positive—Words like *can't, won't, shouldn't,* and *don't* should be used sparingly. Instead of saying, "I can't do that" try "I have a few other options I'd like to get your opinion on." It might be easier for you to explain why you can't accept his offer if you present alternative solutions.

"But"—Think of this word as a cutoff point, beyond which your counterpart will stop listening to what you're saying. He presents his idea, you rephrase it, and immediately you follow up with a "but" statement. For example, "Our production costs are high, but the materials you're requesting are expensive." To the person on the defense, this could sound like you're attacking his original idea by telling him he's wrong to have had it in the first place. Simply remove "but" from the sentence to assure he hears your response: "Production costs are high; the supplier charges X-amount for these materials."

Whenever possible, use facts to back up your objections to the other party's request. Providing evidence for your protest shows him you're not trying to be difficult and helps him better understand your position.

Responding to Stonewalling

The difference between stonewalling and dealing with a difficult person is that the former is a ploy that is purposely used to draw your attention away from the subject you're discussing, while the latter is an innate part of a person's character. To see if the other party is using the tactic, tell him you don't believe he's serious about negotiating with you because he's rejected every offer you've made. Go over your proposals and highlight the points that illustrate how he benefits from them. Then ask him to explain his opposition.

Letting Stress Take Over

Think about the last time you were stressed out. Did your face get red and your palms begin to sweat? Did your heart start to pound rapidly and your body start to shake? Did you get a headache, stomachache, or a nauseous feeling? Now think about what you were doing. Were you shouting or being shouted at? Were you crying? Did you walk out of the room and slam the door? Did you try to injure yourself or someone else? Were you able to think rationally or perform specific duties successfully? Would you have felt comfortable making important decisions at the time you were experiencing stress?

The way you answered these questions will help you cope with stress the next time it appears, particularly during a negotiation.

Unlike substance abuse, stress can be controlled as soon as it appears if you take the time to learn about how it manifests in your world. Once this is done, you can guard against your instinctive, counterproductive reactions and respond with a more constructive approach.

FACT

Stress, like drugs and alcohol, delivers a rush to your brain that affects your body, mind, and spirit to the point of rendering you powerless over your emotions, actions, and ability to think logically.

Know What Sets You Off

Unforgiving negotiators know that the best way to throw other people off course is to tamper with their inner strengths and expose their weaknesses. In other words, they know exactly what buttons to push to upset you. Your first line of defense against this tactic is to know your hot buttons:

- Do you get defensive when your ideas are shot down?
- Do you take it personally when you're verbally attacked?
- Do you get insulted when someone doesn't agree with you?
- Do you get angry when someone rolls his eyes at you?
- Are you easily offended? How so?
- Are you easily intimidated? What are you afraid of?
- How strongly does guilt affect you? Are you quick to give in?

Next, think about how you feel when you're put in similar situations. What emotions do you feel the most? What is your body telling you?

It helps to develop a system for dealing with stress. Go into a quiet room alone and close your eyes for five minutes to regain strength. Take a walk around the block to expend any negative energy. Jot down your favorite quote, a passage from your favorite book, or a saying from your favorite philosopher—anything that helps you feel centered—and read it to yourself when you're feeling overwhelmed. If it's music that relaxes you, take a few minutes to listen to your favorite tune.

Look Both Ways Before Crossing

Not only is this sound advice when on the road, it comes in handy when determining whether you're about to traverse the other party's boundaries and cause even greater irritation. Thinking before reacting is definitely the way to go. Otherwise, you could destroy the relationship by causing more stress, or you could feel defeated by surrendering to it.

If you retaliate with anger, the other party knows she has you right where she wants you: on her territory. Her hardball tactics succeeded in putting you on her level, and now she can use it against you every step of the way. Suddenly, she accuses you of being hard to work with, temperamental, and stubborn. Clearly, this response gets you nowhere and only succeeds in damaging the relationship.

ALERT!

If your response to stressful situations is to take the easy way out and just give in, you're doing yourself a major disservice. Not only do you show the other party how weak you are, but you leave the deal feeling disappointed in yourself because you didn't hold your own. Furthermore, your counterpart will be more than happy to share with his peers his success story of how he got the best of you, a reputation you don't want to acquire.

Mishandling Concessions

Another common pitfall to guard against is the management (or mismanagement) of concessions. In Chapter 1 we discussed when you should make them and when you should ask for them. Here, we'll look at the mistakes that cause you to fall short of important concessions and those that result in your giving up too much. Keep track of the concessions you give and receive; you never know when the tally can be used to influence a decision.

Ask Away

When you sit down to prepare your proposal, you'll have to decide what you think is appropriate and what isn't. From small requests to major ones, write them all down like you can't live without a single one (yes, even if you can!), and highlight the major ones so that you'll remember them when the discussion starts getting more intense. When you get to the negotiating table, check each one off your list as you go along so you don't skip over any.

There's no need to feel greedy or afraid to ask for something you think the other party views as trivial. The truth is, you never know what your counterpart will be willing to agree to. You'll regret it later if with hindsight you realize that the concessions you didn't ask for were things you could have easily gotten.

Aim high even if you think you're aiming too high; your goals might not always be as ambitious as you perceive them to be.

Handing It Over

When it's your turn to give up concessions, one of the biggest mistakes you're liable to make is thinking that the other party values what you're offering as much (or as little) as you do. If your strategy is to offer something you think he wants in exchange for something you really want, the danger lies in the assumption that he will view the trade as being equal. If you take this chance and discover that he doesn't think the deal is fair, he may feel like you're trying to take advantage of him and, as a result, begin withholding concessions.

Avoid making the mistake of offering something small for something big by learning your counterpart's objectives ahead of time. This is especially important when your request would allow you to take a big step closer to reaching your ultimate goal. Make fair offers, and you'll get fair offers.

One more thing to remember about making concessions is that you should always ask for something in return. This point has already been discussed, but it's important enough to mention again—it's easy to make a mistake here. Let's say you give something away without making a request for yourself because you figure you can ask for something later. For now, you'd rather move on to a point you've been eager to discuss. Then "later" comes, and the same situation happens again. If you haven't been keeping track of concessions, you'll fail to see how much you've given away compared to how much you've received. Another drawback is that you'll have to backtrack and re-evaluate the issues under discussion at the time you gave up the concession.

Ask now, not later. Always keep the discussions moving forward and toward the closing, which leads us to the next stumbling block you'll encounter.

Closing Mistakes

The blunders you make during the closing stage can seem a little more drastic than the others we've already discussed. At closing, your negotiations are finalized; once the deal is done, there's no looking back. Before you panic, here are some tips that will restore your calm.

Don't Be Afraid

When re-examining the details of the negotiation, you might come across a miscalculation you made or an inaccuracy in one of your concessions. You may even discover a concession that you didn't mean to make. When this happens, bring it up immediately, even if you feel embarrassed. The longer you wait, the more it will seem like you purposely planted the error as part of a ploy.

In addition to having the courage to point out your own mistakes, you'll need to have the courage to stand up to the other party's last-minute tactics. It's never too late to make changes, even at this stage, but you want to keep them to a minimum because this is when you're trying to get the other party to make commitments. If she asks for an extra concession here and an extra one there, don't give in just to be the good guy and help close the deal faster. Don't worry about being liked during this stage. More importantly, don't be afraid to say "no."

There's Still Time

Making decisions because you feel pressured to do so is one of the worst mistakes you can make, particularly during the closing. Take all the time you need to put the final stamp on the agreements you made, and you'll feel more confident about your decisions later.

While this slower pace may incur the wrath of your counterpart, don't be coerced into finalizing anything you're not ready for. Additionally, know that most deadlines can be negotiated. Even if the extension is just for a few hours, use the extra time efficiently. Go back to the table early if you're able to work out your issues before time is up.

Misjudging Pros and Cons

As you know, using the deadline tactic carries certain risks. It's important to determine whether those risks are worth taking. The same rule applies for any other move you make during a negotiation, whether during the bargaining stage or at closing.

FACT

Risks can be personal or professional, private or social, financial or emotional, and they're all measured differently from one person to the next. For example, you might not feel apprehensive about gambling away your paycheck at the races, but you'd never chance rejection by asking your neighbor out on a date.

If you're worried about your reputation, consider whether you can withstand the ruthlessness of your counterpart. As you're conducting your research, pay close attention to the details that could put you way in over your head financially. Think about how willing you are to put your career on the line and how much you can afford to lose.

On the other hand, if you usually feel intimidated by taking chances that could have an adverse effect on your success, try to build your confidence level. You can start small. For instance, next time you're at the movie theater ordering snacks, ask if you can get a bag of the popcorn that you just saw popping instead of one of the bags that have been sitting on the shelf. Go to a restaurant that's not too busy and ask to sit at a particular table. These small successes will give you the courage to ask for what you want, both in your personal life and at the negotiation table.

One risk you should never feel good about taking is skipping the preparation stage. Your strength comes from knowledge. If you know what you're talking about, you'll feel like you're competent enough to get positive results. You'll also be less likely to back down, which puts not only your self-esteem at risk but also the other party's respect for you.

Keeping Objectives in Focus

There's one last obstacle to watch out for: losing focus. But if you succeed here, you will be better able to keep all your other problems in check. You really can't go wrong if you always have a clear view of your main goals. Whenever you're feeling overwhelmed, anxious, angry, or fed up, simply think about your aspirations, and draw your energy from there. Looking at the big picture makes all the insignificant points fall away.

Remaining goal-oriented also involves memorizing the other party's goals in addition to keeping your own in the forefront. This knowledge gives you leverage and helps you counter the other party's tactics when the time comes. It also reminds the other party, time and time again, that you're working toward solutions that satisfy both your agendas.

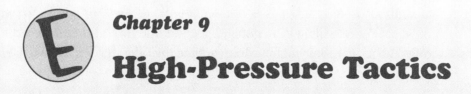

Chapter 9
High-Pressure Tactics

As you discovered in the previous chapter, negotiators use numerous ploys to divert your attention away from the main issues. Similarly, they may engage in high-pressure tactics that force you to make hurried decisions out of fear of losing the deal altogether. These maneuvers can take the form of competitive offers, imaginary deadlines, and ultimatums, leaving little room for negotiation. Once you learn how to counter these tactics, you'll discover that you have more room than you think.

Unrealistic First Offer

One way to get a "feel" for how much (or how little) the other party is willing to give you is by giving an unrealistic first offer. The other party's reaction to this offer can prove to be very useful. First, based on their expression—anger, dissatisfaction, surprise, composure, or eagerness—you can get an idea about what number is either acceptable to them or within the scope of what they're willing to negotiate. Second, the more unrealistic your first offer, the more room you have to negotiate the offer that you're really willing to settle on.

Offending the Other Party

Sometimes the other party takes offense to this kind of tactic, especially if she is well prepared and has researched the market to come up with her own number. You can avoid making the situation uncomfortable by gathering as much information as you can about the other party's disposition before the negotiation is held. If her knowledge is extensive in the subject or if she has several alternatives, don't start off too far off the mark. She'll be aware of what you're doing and it might backfire.

Before you make conclusions about the other party's reaction to your unrealistic offer, determine whether the emotions he displays are sincere. One way he can counter is by feigning shock or insult in an effort to get you to lower your initial offer.

The other party's surprised reaction to your offer might also be an indication of whether she has a back-up plan. Her strong response could be an attempt to get a better offer than the one she already has (or thinks she can get) from someone else.

Practice Prevention

You can avoid getting an unrealistic offer from the other party by making sure that you are the one who makes an offer first. This strategy will also enable you to secure the starting point from which you'll be negotiating. If the other party beats you to it, however, remember to keep your cool. Even though you might be quite satisfied with the offer, be careful not to show your satisfaction. She might realize her mistake and try to make up for it later when you're discussing a different issue.

Another way to counter the other party's unrealistic offer is to ignore it completely. Start talking about something else to tactfully deliver the message that you're not happy with the offer.

If you do intend to make the first offer, be careful not to put yourself at a disadvantage. If you're not sure of the rules of the game, you may err on the side of caution. Your offer might be less to your advantage than the one the other party had intended to make.

"One Time Only" Offer

Remember all that time and effort you put into preparing yourself for this negotiation? Well, don't let it all go to waste by succumbing to a phony take-it-or-leave-it tactic that turns your hard work into something that was done in vain. This is a common ploy meant to make you feel like there's an enormous amount of pressure on you to close the deal quickly.

ALERT!

Never, never, never make a decision you're not ready to make, especially when the other party makes you feel like you're under the gun. If you're like most people, you don't respond well to pressure. Have you ever forgotten the one thing you were supposed to take with you to the office the next morning because you were so late you were literally running out the door?

We simply do not perform at our best in high-pressure situations; our thought process speeds up to such a rate that there isn't enough time to think things through. When a negotiator approaches you with a "one time only" offer, he's trying to catch you off guard and is most likely bluffing. By telling you, for example, that you have two hours to make a decision, he's not giving you the appropriate amount of time to do additional research, consult your team, or weigh the pros and cons of the situation. You're also not given the chance to ask important questions or reassess your goals and objectives.

Ignore the Tactic

When the other party introduces this tactic into the discussion, ignore it. Continue talking about the issues that were brought up or start talking about other ones. Remember, he's only trying to intimidate you. Show him you won't be manipulated in this way by refusing to acknowledge his insistent request.

In some cases, the other party's speech will speed up considerably. He might begin to talk fast and make short, blunt statements to emphasize his point even further. Don't let yourself be bulldozed; slow him down, ask questions, and most importantly don't be forced into closing a deal if you're not ready.

The Real Deal

On rare occasions when the other party really is in a crunch for time, try to get an extension on the deadline. Whether it's for an extra day or for an extra week, any additional length of time will give you the opportunity to weigh your alternatives and re-examine your goals to see if they're being met.

If your requests for more time are denied, let the other party know what your concerns are, and try to develop specific solutions that help eliminate the need for a deadline. At this point in the discussion, if the other party still continues to impose a strict deadline on you, show them that you won't be pressured into making overnight decisions by calling off the negotiation.

Game Delay

The opposite of the deadline ploy is the delay tactic. Delay tactics are used by negotiators in a variety of ways: to stall, to test your urgency, or to temporarily appease you. It's okay to give the other party some time to absorb everything so they feel comfortable about the decisions they're about to make, but set a limit. Don't let them take advantage of you.

FACT

Some negotiators purposely ask for a delay so they can mull everything over for a while before making the commitment. This delay should be no more than two days, and they should tell you up front how much time they need. If you've traveled quite a distance to meet with them, two to three hours should be sufficient.

Stalling Negotiations

Stalling brings negotiations to a halt. By digging her heels in the ground, the other party decides she simply cannot go any further because your requests are unacceptable. Naturally, you'll begin to think about what concessions you can offer in order to keep the negotiation moving forward. However, before you start thinking about whether you can be a little more flexible with your concessions, ask her point blank what she would consider to be acceptable. Find out exactly what the obstructing element is, and try to work the issue out before you give her anything more.

Testing Urgency

You'll want to be careful about how you react to the other party's delay because there may be only one reason he's using it: to see how desperate you are for his business. It may seem like a silly cat-and-mouse game, but sometimes you have no choice but to play along. When you do, it'll go something like this. The other party calls for a delay, you agree, then nothing happens. No phone calls. No e-mails. No contact of any kind. If you initiate contact, say the next day, the other party will know that you have no alternatives, that he has the upper hand, and that he can get more concessions out of you.

As tough as it might be, you really need to wait this one out and let him come to you. Even more difficult is determining how long you should wait for a response. While you don't want to seem eager, you don't want to let too many days slip by without hearing a word.

If you feel secure with the other options you have in place, make contact after a few days and let him know you're not happy with what he's doing. Motivate him to give you a decision by giving him a deadline; tell him all deals are off the table if you don't have his answer by a specified time.

The Check Is in the Mail

We've all heard that one before! Somewhere on a continent still to be discovered, there stands a mailbox, overstuffed with all those checks that somehow had the wrong addresses on them.

This six-word phrase was designed to give the person on the receiving end a false sense of security. A negotiator uses this tactical delay not to pressure you but to take the pressure off himself and buy more time to fulfill his obligation.

Sometimes the system is slow (checks are processed elsewhere and therefore take awhile to be drawn), and there's nothing anybody can do about it. If you've experienced this over and over again with the same company, let them know you're not a pushover by finding something to take away from them (the report you promised, the early shipment you said you'd arrange) until they deliver.

If your mailbox is still empty (and you haven't had the good fortune to find the lost continent), take action! Visit the other party or the company you've been doing business with to say that you refuse to leave until they pay up. Sometimes legal action is necessary, but usually things can be worked out so they don't get to that point.

Remember to use your backup plan as leverage. Tell the other party you have another option that you plan to pursue if he can't reach a decision. Don't be aggressive, but do make him aware that you're giving him the first opportunity and you have to have a commitment from him soon.

The Bottom Line

Some negotiators love to use a bogus bottom line—a point beyond which the deal is not negotiable. For example, the person you're negotiating with might say that her supervisor will not allow her to decrease the price lower than a certain number. Giving a false bottom line is a way to avoid having to negotiate many concessions, and it can be used in just about any situation.

The way to face this gambit is to call attention away from the bottom-line number by focusing on the topics that interest your opponent the most. Whenever the other party zeros in on one particular issue—in this case, price—get her to stop looking at problems with tunnel vision and start examining the negotiation as a whole. In this instance, if you start talking about something you have that she wants, she'll start thinking in terms of how the two of you can find a solution that allows each of you to walk away with something.

Splitting the Difference

This is perhaps the quickest way for a negotiator to sell out in his field of expertise. It goes against the basic principles of negotiating because it's almost like taking the lazy way out. Why acquire all that skill if you're just going to let it go to waste? This is how splitting the difference works: You have a number—say, $100,000—and your counterpart has a number—say it's $92,000—and neither one of you wants to move. Someone suggests splitting the difference and calling it even—$8,000 is the difference between the two numbers and split two ways is $4,000. This means the agreed offer would be $96,000.

If you're like most, you might think that's a fair trade, a wonderful solution to a difficult situation—a compromise. Actually, you're misinterpreting the operative meaning of this phrase. True, splitting the difference is a compromise, but it's not as straightforward as it sounds. Just because it expedites the solution to a problem you're struggling with, this technique will not necessarily satisfy your goals and objectives in the long run.

At first glance, it seems as though agreeing on $96,000 is a legitimate concession. Look again, and you'll discover that it actually works like this. If you agree to split the difference, but the product you're selling is worth more than $96,000, you are at a loss. On the other hand, if it's worth less than $96,000, the other person loses. Even though you're splitting the difference of your initial offers, it's not always the best thing to do if the resulting number makes one person's situation better than the other's.

Every issue deserves to be negotiated efficiently and proactively, and splitting the difference does not promote that. The same holds true when you realize how many times a number can be split, and how often this tactic is used.

Crunching the Numbers

Another misconception about splitting the difference is that it's always a fifty-fifty result. This misguided idea doesn't take into account that a number can be split several times. Let's say your offer is $100,000 and the other person's is $75,000. He suggests you split the difference and settle at $87,500. Three major events just took place here:

1. You have your counterpart's new number ($87,500).
2. A new range has been established ($100,000 to $87,500).
3. You didn't make the offer.

Since the other party has set the new price at $87,500, you can now negotiate within a range of $100,000 (your original offer) and $87,500 (his new offer). If you split the difference and instead come down a little bit with an offer of $95,000 by saying, "I can't go down to $87,500 but I can do $95,000." The range has just shifted again to $95,000 to $87,500. Then you insinuate another split by letting the other party think that he came up with the suggestion.

FACT

Continuously alluding to another split with statements like, "We're so close to having an agreement, it would be a shame to let it go for a measly $7,500" should provoke the other party into suggesting another split, in which the new range would be $95,000 to $91,250. Now you're even closer in number than you were before, thus in a better position to hint at another split.

Analyze the Tactic

When you take a closer look at the "splitting the difference" scenario, you can see that, if applied correctly, this gambit can be used to your advantage. You'll notice that you only came down on your original offer of $100,000 by $5,000 while your counterpart went up a whopping $16,250 from $75,000. While this example is extreme, you can get the idea of how "splitting the difference" really is a deceptive solution.

False Concessions

Let's say you walk into a store to look at the gorgeous jacket you saw in the window. A salesperson approaches you and says, "The jacket costs $75, but for you, I'll sell it for $65." She wants to let you know up front that she's giving you the deal of the century on this thing. You smile politely and go back to the jacket to look over the pockets and buttons, when suddenly she says, "Ok, it seems you really like this jacket so I'll give it to you for $55." Another discount? Now you're really interested! You inquire about the fiber content, wash instructions, and so on, and the salesperson reduces the price another $10. Feeling like you just hit the jackpot, you pay for the jacket and leave a satisfied customer. Five minutes later another prospective customer walks into the store and starts looking at the jacket, wherein the keen salesperson says, "The jacket costs $85, but for you, I'll sell it for $75."

In both instances, the seller had a set figure in her mind the whole time. By exaggerating the price and then handing out a few concessions, she made it seem like you got a great bargain right there on the spot.

Retailers often use the "exaggerated first offer" tactic in conjunction with the multiple concessions tactic to make a larger, more expensive item seem more attractive by including smaller, equally gratifying items: "When you buy this advanced treadmill, you also receive our latest exercise video and a free bottle of multi-vitamins."

When you encounter a situation in which a concession is made at the onset of a negotiation, there are a few things to be aware of before you make a decision. Is the seller asking for anything in return? If not, chances are that it's not a real concession. Is the dollar amount being significantly lowered or are you given a range? If the salesperson has switched to a price range, chances are she won't come down in price beyond the range offer.

Using Competition As Leverage

This tactic works extremely well when trying to decide which cell-phone carrier to subscribe to. Call several wireless companies to hear each of their offers, then go back to the one with the most attractive offer and mention that you are also looking into such-and-such company and were quoted a rate that you're seriously considering. Nine times out of ten, you'll get another offer right away. Continue doing this until the best deal presents itself.

Now let's say the roles flip, and your opponent is the one with several other options. He is out looking for the best offer, and he won't hesitate to let you know it. Be careful. You don't know for a fact that your competitors have made better offers, and there's a chance this guy is bluffing. If you encounter a situation like this, get the other party to talk about what they like about your product or what they don't like about your competitor's product. If you can offer something that the others can't, then you have gained some of your leverage back. Using timing and deadlines is another way to make your offer more attractive.

Chapter 10

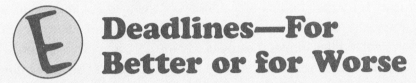

Deadlines—For Better or for Worse

Our lives would be so much easier without the pressure of deadlines. We could work at a relaxed pace and forego late nights at the office forever. Isn't that a nice thought? Now think about what life would be like without the help of deadlines: the warehouse that ships your products to your customers only does so once every three weeks; your mechanic gets around to fixing your car whenever the mood strikes him. As you can see, deadlines make life complicated, but they also help us get things done.

Dealing with Deadlines

Certainly you've seen that busy mother at the grocery store. She's got an infant in one of her arms and a toddler pulling on her other arm, begging her to get the double chocolate-chip cookies. The infant wails incessantly, and the toddler whines while the mother tries to get items that are on her grocery list. After about twenty minutes of trying to comfort the infant and ignoring the toddler's pleas, the mother is at her wit's end. She gives in to the persistent toddler, throws the cookies in the cart, and takes a deep breath.

While the requests from your counterpart might not be as vocalized as a toddler's, his intent is the same—to catch you at your weakest moment and cash in on it by asking for concessions. Typically (and this is what the other party is betting on), we're more apt to agree to compromise when we're experiencing time restraints. When too much is coming at us all at once, it's easier to get rid of the most immediate, stressful factor, and then take the time to work it out. In the previous example, the mother knew it would take a while to comfort her newborn, and she knew her toddler wouldn't give up until she got her way. In a matter of seconds, the toddler was appeased and the mother could relax a little and focus on pacifying the newborn.

ALERT!

A problem arises when both parties share the same deadline. Only one of you can have the upper hand. Whoever has the most alternatives has the most control over the negotiation. The weaker party should be aware of this and try to complete negotiations well before the due date.

The last-minute offer is another method the other party uses to try to effortlessly sway your decision. For example, if the lease is almost up on your apartment, the landlord will wait until the end of the month to inform you of the rate increase because he assumes you haven't decided to move out and will need to extend the lease. Similarly, you might hold out on informing the landlord of your decision to stay because you assume no one else is interested in the apartment since you haven't made any indication of leaving.

Although most leases have a thirty-day notice written into their contracts, this example illustrates how important leverage is. If you wait until the last minute to keep your apartment, you can almost guarantee the landlord has three interested parties lined up, all willing to accept a higher price.

Quick Settlements

In his book *Friendly Persuasion: My Life As a Negotiator,* Bob Woolf encourages readers not to worry about agreeing with the other party to settle a negotiation promptly if the offer is nonpartisan. It could be that your counterpart has a lot on her plate and wants to conduct an honest, yet efficient, negotiation so she can tend to the rest of his pressing business matters. Just because the negotiation process doesn't take all day doesn't mean you're not walking away with a good deal.

It's all a matter of doing research—every step along the negotiating path relies heavily on your efforts to lay the groundwork during the preparation stage. The quality of information you uncover affects your success from beginning to end. If you've done your homework, relax. Build your strength from there. You'll find that you're confident enough to recognize when a decent offer comes your way—regardless of how long it takes to reach an agreement.

Withholding Information

Sometimes the other party will wait until the deadline is near to disclose additional information, leaving you little time to digest the new details. She wants to see how far you'll bend and are hoping that, like the mother in the grocery store, you're too frazzled to put your best foot forward. This is a tough one to face with composure, but you can and will get through it if you never lose sight of your initial goals.

No matter how long the negotiation has taken thus far or how drained you feel, counter this ploy with every last ounce of energy you have, if on principle alone. Ask questions; go over your notes; reassess your goals; ask for concessions; consult other members on your team; ask for more time; and if all else fails, end negotiations. Just don't give in, and more importantly, don't give up.

Real or Imaginary?

On a day-to-day basis, you encounter very real deadlines—like those at work, at your children's school, or with your budget. These deadlines are clearly defined and easy to recognize. But how do you tell if a deadline proposed by the other negotiating party is real? This section will help you identify imaginary deadlines and tell you how to tackle them.

How to Tell the Difference

One approach is to use a formula that combines what you already know about your counterpart with what you can assess from his delivery of the transaction. If, throughout the course of your research, you discovered the other party has a history of using unfair tactics, employing an intimidating style of negotiating, and being hard to work with, re-examine how he conveyed the deadline information to you. If he was demanding, you can almost be sure his deadline is imaginary.

To test if your assumption is accurate, ask your counterpart a series of questions. His response not only answers the questions you asked him, they answer the questions you're asking yourself:

- "Why is this deadline necessary?" answers your internal question, "Is this a real deadline?"
- "Is this deadline the best option?" answers your internal question, "How does the other party benefit from this deadline?"
- "What are the consequences if I don't accept this deadline?" answers your internal question, "What do I stand to lose if I refuse to comply?"

If the answers you receive do not justify the need for a deadline, then ask for an extension. Just like anything else, deadlines are negotiable. They should not be used as a means of pressuring you to make decisions in haste. If the other party still will not budge, put the focus on objectives. This way, the issue can transition into something more goal-oriented.

Watch Out

If you've got a deadline in mind, don't communicate it to the other party. Putting her in the know about your 8:00 P.M. flight gives her the opportunity to use the time limit to her advantage. For instance, she can save the most important issues until the very end because she anticipates that you will give up a lot more than you intended to make it to the gate on time.

If you inadvertently divulge your deadline, consider what the other party doesn't know—maybe you're just as willing to get on a later flight or even stay overnight in a hotel if it means hammering out the details to come to an agreement.

Another mousetrap to sidestep is a statement like, "Let's agree to this now, but save the details for later; I'm pressed for time today." The truth is, the other party hopes you'll forget about the agreement you made so he can work out the details in his favor and later on remind you how you were in agreement with him. Make certain you have every detail about the agreement right then and there to prevent this from happening. If he's persistent, tell him you want it to go on record that you did not make an agreement on this matter, and make a note to yourself about it in case he still tries to get away with it later.

Deadlines carry the possibility that nobody will come out a winner, such as when workers go on strike or if an athlete reaches the end of his contract. Keep in mind that the other party's deadline is not yours, and you should not feel pressured into accepting it as such. Likewise, if you have a schedule you'd like to stick to, work with your counterpart to negotiate a new deadline that combines both your needs.

When the Time Is Right

If there really is a time and place for everything, the elements of negotiating are no exception to the rule. Now that you're aware of many of the tactics expert negotiators use, it's good to know when to expect them. Though they can be used at any point in the discussion, there are a few key moments when you can be particularly sure your guard is up and your awareness is on.

Perfect Timing

Be on the lookout for pressure tactics that are couched with concessions. For example, the other party asks to have the first shipment of 1,000 pieces delivered by the end of the month. Before you decide on when the first shipment will arrive, you need to work out what it will include. If you haven't decided on how many pieces the first shipment will contain, tell your counterpart you'd like to keep things simple by negotiating one concession at a time. An oversight like this could end up costing you two concessions for his one.

Similarly, if you inquire about a topic and your counterpart immediately calls for a caucus (a closed meeting among his associates), look for signs that suggest he's bluffing in order to make the topic hold more weight than it actually does. Continue to ask questions that test the validity of this showcase; ask him outright what details are giving him the most trouble with the issue.

Think Differently

Sometimes no one wants to make a move at the beginning of a negotiation, especially if both parties are so well matched; they're employing the same tactics at the same time to achieve similar results. If the other party agrees to give you a concession, say a free five-year warranty, in exchange for your making the first offer, listen very carefully for the alarm that should be sounding in your head.

Sure, the warranty deal sounds attractive enough, but no matter what offer you make, your counterpart is likely to say, "You can't be serious. How can I justify giving you a free warranty after you've given me a figure like that?" His plan worked, and now the offer you fought so hard to protect is wide open for his attacks.

The Value of Limitations

Though it's more common for deadlines to be used against you, there are ways to use them in your favor. One of the most discouraging aspects of a negotiation is feeling like you're getting nowhere. If the other party is stalling and you're ready to move on, circle back to the focus of the discussion by instituting a deadline that causes her to spring back into action. Make it apparent that she's in danger of losing your business if she doesn't give you a decision by a specified time and date, at which point all deals will be off. Remember, work toward both your and the other party's goals, but don't allow her to push you around.

If two of your other alternatives have already made you offers, take advantage of setting a deadline that urges the party you're dealing with now to make an offer before the others expire and you're no longer able to compare all three. Be considerate when presenting the limitation so as not to offend the other person, and just give her the facts: "I hope I can have your offer today because I'm expecting two others this evening."

ALERT!

There's no easy way to deliver a deadline without causing the other party to be a little miffed. No matter how gently you approach the subject, she's going to get upset because you're putting her in a compromising position. However, your use of tact when making the request will not cause her to feel pressured by a demand.

Use the other party's deadline as a reference point when building a case against it. It sounds a little odd, but it works. If you haven't already conceded to a few of the other party's requests, get away from the deadline issue and start hitting on some minor points and maybe even one or two major ones. The idea is to give the other party some of what she wants so the next time she brings up the deadline, you can illustrate how it prevents you from being able to make your concessions happen for her. To put it simply, tell her you cannot meet her shipment deadlines *and* get the warehouse to honor a discount. Money speaks volumes; make it speak loud and clear for you.

Measure the Risks

Now that you know how deadlines can help you, let's find out how they can hurt you if your plan backfires. Before you consider using the deadline tactic, determine what possible repercussions could ensue and whether the gamble is worth taking. If the consequences outweigh the benefits, think of another strategy to implement.

Think about how your deadline is going to make the other person feel. Based on your research and observations of her negotiating characteristics so far, you should be able to predict whether she'll feel intimidated, offended, frustrated, manipulated, or confused. The ability to read your counterpart is a godsend. The basic fundamentals to acquiring this skill are discussed in-depth in the next chapter.

QUESTION?

How do I know whether the other party is faking it?

If your counterpart's reaction to the deadline seems to be out of step with how she's reacted to previous requests, try to understand the motivation behind her response by asking questions that will reveal her true concerns: "What problems does this present for you? Is there a time frame you would suggest?" Pay attention to how defensive she gets after you ask each question. Liars don't like being exposed.

Waiting It Out

Most concessions are made toward the end of a negotiation's deadline, if there is one. The explanation is simple. The more time the two parties invest in the negotiation process, the less likely they will be to pull out. If one party begins demanding new concessions, the opponents are more likely to give in so that negotiations can come to a successful end. However, sitting tight until the end and then asking for additional concessions is a high-risk strategy, and you will need patience and self-confidence to use it.

Your counterpart is aware of this strategy, and it is quite likely he'll try to use it. When he does, counter the tactic by examining his position:

- What is his motivation?
- Is he trying to buy time, and if so, why?
- What does he hope to achieve?
- What does he stand to lose?
- If you opt out, how does that affect his plan?
- Does he have a hidden agenda?

The amount of patience you have is truly put to the test when two equally attractive offers are presented to you. If you're a musician negotiating a record contract and company A offers you a generous monetary advance while company B offers you a higher percentage in royalties, which one do you choose? While a large sum of cash could get you out of debt now, if you have the misfortune of becoming a one-hit wonder, you'll be thankful you went with the second option.

Another way to use patience as a tactic—one that's not so chancy—is to acquire more time to conduct additional research. If you have drawn a number of conclusions about your counterpart or speculated why the company he works for is putting pressure on him to close the deal, it's in your best interest to dig a little deeper to test your assumptions. You might be surprised to discover just how important your deal is to them.

When the eleventh hour rolls around, don't be opposed to extending the negotiation if it means the best deal can be worked out if given more time.

Chapter 11

Relying on Body Language

S ometimes the most important conversation you can have with another
person involves no words at all. Becoming
fluent in body language requires a great
deal of time, effort, practice, and applica-
tion, but it's worth the effort—honing your
body language skills will help you uncover
hidden agendas, discover a person's true
feelings, gain insight into someone's character, predict reactions, and become aware
of your own nonverbal behavior.

Unconscious Behavior

The challenge of reading body language lies in how misleading it can be. It's not an exact science, and many nonverbal cues can be interpreted in numerous ways. Even though there are some standard generalizations, each signal is unique to the person and the context. Most of the time we don't know our bodies are silently communicating with the rest of the world; even if even we did, we probably wouldn't know what we were saying.

Speaking body language is instinctive. People don't consciously move their arms when they speak—it just happens. It's natural for arms to move, feet to tap, and eyes to turn away when engaged in verbal conversation. In fact, it feels very unnatural to carry out these behaviors consciously. Because it's awkward to make your body go against its own grain, these skills must be learned and developed over time in order to execute them with the level of sophistication needed to make the act seem effortless.

FACT

The ability to control body language is an important part of being an actor. A good actor really knows how to employ this silent language to show how the character is feeling.

It's useful to observe how body language is used in conjunction with speech. After you gain some experience with this, you'll realize that nonverbal cues can either emphasize the spoken words or undermine them. For example, if a person says he's satisfied with your offer, but grips his pen and clenches his fist as he says so, you might ask yourself if he's really unhappy with the offer. To test this assumption, ask a few questions to see if he can open up and tell you how he really feels.

There are literally thousands of nonverbal cues to discover, not to mention thousands of ways to interpret them, and we simply do not have the room to list them all here. The following table covers some of the most common nonverbal cues and their functions.

Common Nonverbal Cues

Body Language	Possible Meaning
Crossed arms	Defensive, immovable, opposing
Crossed legs, ankles	Competitive, opposing
Clenched hands, strong grip on object	Frustration
Cocked head	Interested, attentive
Covering mouth with hands	Dishonesty
Fidgeting	Apprehensive, unconfident
Finger tapping or drumming	Boredom
Frequent nodding	Eagerness
Hand-steepling (forming church)	Confidence
Hands on hips	Confidence, impatience
Hands on cheek, chin, or glasses	Thinking, examining
Hands on table or desk	Poise
Head in hand	Disinterested, disrespectful
Leaning forward	Enthusiasm
Open arms, hands	Open-minded, approachable
Perpetual eye blinking	Deception
Rubbing nose, forehead	Uptight, confrontational
Side glance	Suspicion
Sitting on edge of seat	Prepared, enthusiastic
Slouching, leaning back	Challenging, rejecting
Throat-clearing	Nervousness

Spend time getting the basics down before you move on to the more complicated cues, such as breathing, which can be tricky to recognize at first due to its subtle nature. Jot down notes about the other party's body language each time an issue is discussed so you can analyze it later if you don't have time to do it on the spot.

Facial Expressions

Evolution has afforded us the ability to develop a wide range of social behaviors, including the resourcefulness of communicating a message with just a single look. As soon as we meet someone for the first time, we begin sizing them up and immediately try to find clues that allude to their character so we can get a general idea of what kind of person we are dealing with.

FACT

Facial expressions summarize a person's disposition and, because of that, prove to be invaluable tools throughout the course of a negotiation. Some signs to look out for include: raised eyebrows (uncertainty, concern); nose-scratching (confusion); widening of the eyes (surprise, disbelief, anxiety); and minor eye-squinting (contemplative, questioning).

Upon first meeting someone, the first thing you do is look at the person's face. Eye contact is made, smiles are exchanged, and a slight nod of approval might be reciprocated. Based on this initial meeting, it's easy to assume the other person is friendly, outgoing, respectful, and considerate because she has made a good first impression on you. Likewise, if the person looks off to the side instead of at you, barely smiles, and keeps her hands tucked in her pockets, you're inclined to believe this person to be unfriendly, unhappy, rude, and cold.

Vocalization

Your voice is instrumental in expressing how you feel. Tone, tempo, and cadence play as crucial a role as word choice in communication. Use your voice to get your point across more effectively, to get someone's attention, to sooth or calm someone who's upset, or to gain insight into your counterpart's intentions.

Tone is comprised of many elements: pitch (high or low frequency), stress (emphasis), and volume (loudness) are the elements you need to monitor. It is used to place importance on certain words, and if not done correctly, your counterpart can totally misread your meaning and emotionality. Consider the following example, where bold face indicates emphasis on a particular word:

- **What** do you want?
- What **do** you want?
- What do **you** want?
- What do you **want**?

Notice how the meaning of each question is changed depending on where the emphasis is? If it's still unclear, read each one out loud with the proper inflection and think about how you would react in each situation.

ALERT!

Loud tones can be used to get someone's attention or to make a point, but they may sound threatening and filled with anger. Soft, quiet tones make people feel relaxed and safe, but they may also signal weakness and be ignored.

Tempo refers to how fast you speak (rushing through sentences or slow and calculated), while cadence is the rhythm or style of your voice (dull monotone or exciting variations). If your counterpart is speaking too fast, he may be nervous or apprehensive about something. If his voice drones on without any use of tone or pitch, he may be uninterested or distracted by something.

Unconscious Movements

Facial expressions and vocal notes are important, but you can also tell a lot just from watching body movements. When you're disputing something or are talking about something you're excited about, your hands move just as much as your mouth does!

The most effective public speakers, the ones who are memorable months after you attended their seminar, know the secret to keeping the audience's attention is to use their bodies to get their messages across. Whether they're on stage in front of hundreds of people or at the front of a small audience of about twenty, they will use everything they have on the outside (head, face, arms, and legs) to give you everything they have on the inside (personality, excitement, passion, intelligence, experience).

To get a new perspective during a discussion, try changing your position in the room by getting out of your seat to stand by the window. Next, walk across the room and stand at the other side of the table. When you're ready to sit back down, choose a different seat. Each physical change you make can incite a new idea or a new way of thinking.

Universal Gestures

A funny thing happened as human beings evolved. All across the board, we somehow managed to develop a few of the same gesticulations. As a result, there are thousands of books, articles, theories, reports, experiments, and tests—all designed to explain this phenomenon. To illustrate a few of the more fascinating results of this data, let's look at how learned behaviors can influence the success of your negotiations abroad.

Transcending the Language Barrier

No matter how different the human race is among its cultures, beliefs, spoken languages, traditions, and individuals, there are some things we all have in common when it comes to expressing ourselves. At birth, we instinctively know that crying brings comfort; as adults, when we see someone laughing we know they are happy.

Greetings, Earthling

If your negotiations take place in another country, take the time to learn a few polite expressions and how they are relayed. Greetings indicate respect and affection and what better way to express those things to someone than in their native tongue. You can be sure they're doing their part to make you feel more comfortable on their turf.

A concentrated study about the country you're visiting should be done during the preparation phase of the negotiation. However, here's a sample of how to say hello in Asia:

- China—nod and/or bow
- Japan—put your heels together, palms on the sides of your thighs, and bow
- Sri Lanka—press your palms together under your chin and bow

ALERT!

As a tourist, you may use pantomime so the natives can understand you, but avoid using gestures if you don't know what they mean to the people in the country you're visiting. For example, the "A-OK" hand signal where the thumb and index finger meet to form a circle, is very offensive in some countries, as is the sign for "We are #1."

Dress for Success

How you choose to dress says a lot about who you are. If you plan on pursuing a career in the business world, you'll need to dress in appropriate business attire. People who respect the game show it by looking the part, and frankly, they get more respect for doing so. Would you expect a football player to wear anything other than his team uniform? While not all professions have adopted a standard way of dressing, the business world has, and the reasons are justifiable. Fortunately, there's no need to sacrifice style for a professional look; just follow a few simple rules and you'll be ready for the executive runway in no time.

For men, a good rule of thumb is to stick with dark blue or gray suits. Black is acceptable, but looks a little morbid; you can offset this with pinstripes. A crisp shirt, complementary tie, and polished, scratch-free dress shoes are also important. For women, the same rules apply, and you have the options of a blouse and a skirted suit to add to your wardrobe. Keep heels at or below two inches, and wear nylons. Soft, muted hues such as beige, taupe, white, or tan work well, but darker colors project more authority.

People who hold reputable positions tend to dress conservatively to project an air of importance, status, and intelligence. This in turn allows the other party to place confidence in the businessperson's abilities to perform his job well. If you hired an accountant to carefully manage your $2.5-million lottery winnings, how would you feel if he greeted you in a ripped T-shirt, khakis, and sandals?

Mirroring Your Counterpart

An effective way to build trust with the other party is to repeat their style of speaking, tone of voice, and posture. If done with skill (without seeming to mimic the other person), your counterpart will feel like you truly understand him, and a foundation for open communication will be established. Because most of us have a tendency to favor one sense over the other, the statements we make reflect this choice and help in determining how to follow the other party's lead. These statements will generally fall into one of three of the following categories: visual attributes, auditory forms, or kinesics.

The basis of a good handshake is to be confident, reassuring, and quick about it. The space between your thumb and index finger should be positioned in the same exact spot on the other person's hand. Once contact is made, use the rest of your fingers to gently but firmly press the other person's hand as you bring it down to pump once or twice. Make eye contact, then let go of the hand.

Visual Attributes

People who prefer to understand their world from a mostly visual perspective respond to color, shapes, graphic design elements, and physical movements. They make statements like, "It seems clear from my point of view" and "I see where you're coming from." Try to relate to these people by using similar statements that incorporate visual elements into the sentence, "It looks good to me."

Auditory Forms

As the title suggest, these people are attuned to a world of sounds. They tend to hear before they see, and they recall memories by first describing the sounds they remember during that moment in time. They are keen on observing tone and the sounds of movement (slamming doors, sighs of frustration). Their statements include, "It sounds good to me," "I hear what you're saying," and "I don't have to listen to this."

A Study of Kinesics

Kinesthetic people are very object-oriented. They usually need one to "get a handle on the situation" or "grasp the point you're trying to make." It's easy to pick up on their clues because "in light of" how many times you propose your offer, they just can't seem to "come to grips with it." Is any of this starting to "ring a bell"?

Reading and Sending Appropriate Signals

As you can see, body language isn't quick and easy. You really need to look at the whole picture in order to get a true read on someone. And there's always the possibility that you misunderstand something. Reading body language is all guesswork; no one can ever be 100-percent sure about what they think the other person's intentions are. Nevertheless, there are a few techniques that help you recognize patterns and inconsistencies in the other party as well as within yourself.

The Body Language Litmus Test

At the beginning of a negotiation, you and your counterpart will exchange friendly, chatty conversation as a way of getting to know each other. During this process, get to know his nonverbal personality as well. Look for breathing patterns, nuances, and idiosyncrasies; notice if he smiles a lot, grins, or smirks; try to assess his attitude by listening for tone and watching how often he makes eye contact. Once you've committed these impressions to memory, use them as a means of comparison once negotiations begin.

Get your counterpart to talk about something he's happy about—like his significant other, children, pets, or cars. Since he's not pretending to be happy about his favorite things, you can make accurate notes about his body language while he's talking about Scruffy, and look for those cues again later.

Who's Bluffing?

The best way to tell if someone is bluffing during a negotiation is to ask questions. If you recognize nonverbal cues that suggest your counterpart is bluffing, put him to the test by poking around to see what you can dig up. As the previous chapters suggest, information is your most powerful tool, and it usually throws the other party off guard if you ask them to back up their statements.

Take a Look in the Mirror

If you want to be sure you're sending the right signals, one way to do it is to videotape yourself giving a couple of speeches (even if it's a birthday speech or toast to your best friend) and review the tape often. You can also ask family members and friends how they perceive your body language. Ultimately, the only sure way to know what you're revealing is to perfect your poker face in front of the mirror and practice using it.

Using and Interpreting Silence

A quote from twentieth-century French composer Claude Debussy sums up the power of silence beautifully: "Music is the silence between the notes." This statement illustrates how important the stillness becomes in relation to how much of an impact the music will deliver. The same holds true while negotiating.

It Goes Without Saying

It's amazing how much a person is willing to reveal when you exercise your right to be quiet. Some people are unnerved by long periods of silence and feel the need to say anything just to alleviate the discomfort they feel. This is usually when information you didn't have previously falls right into your lap.

It's also a great way to give your counterpart a chance to voice something he's been waiting for the right moment to say. He'll appreciate that you're not trying to take over the conversation by affording him the opportunity. Say nothing, and let it all happen. It's that simple.

Another way to use silence to your advantage is to put pressure on the other party. Sometimes it'll be misinterpreted as a bad sign by those who don't know any better, but in the game of "He who speaks first loses," it'll work in your favor when the other party relinquishes his position of power.

Calm Before the Storm

In the throes of a heated argument, you need to be careful you don't say something that could damage your credibility or ruin the relationship you spent so long nurturing with your counterpart. If you feel things are getting out of control and there's a danger you might misspeak, stop talking. Let the other party continue to rant—he'll stop after he realizes you're not arguing with him anymore. Use the opportunity to determine your next move before another word is spoken.

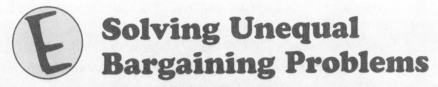

Chapter 12

Solving Unequal Bargaining Problems

argaining power is dependent on an endless number of components, all of which work together to create the leverage you will use during the negotiating process. The biggest misconception about bargaining power is that one side has more of it than the other side. The truth is, both sides have strengths and weaknesses that should be acknowledged by both parties and used to their advantage to create solutions that work all around the table.

When You're the Underdog

Let's say the other party has a prestigious reputation, is a long-acknowledged expert on the subject of your discussion, has superior negotiating skills, and has a stellar team backing him up. You have none of these advantages. This makes you the underdog in the negotiations. You can still do well, but you'll need to do a lot of research and put in a lot of time and determination into the negotiation.

Don't let yourself be intimidated by all those credentials. Use this book to empower yourself. You'll start to believe in yourself and your abilities, and the other party will seem less threatening to you.

As you go through the preparation stage of negotiating, be aware of where you can acquire leverage. Study your counterpart's competition by looking for ways they can both damage and help her. If any of your concessions can give the other party a jump on her competition, that's a plus on your side. Map out a plan on how you can use this concession as a source of strength, what you're willing to give up for it, and whether your counterpart can do without it or bargain for it with one of her other alternatives. If you are the only person who is able to give her what she wants, you have more of an advantage than you thought.

Your goal is to walk into the negotiation as if you couldn't possibly fail. Give yourself the momentum of an experienced negotiator by toughening up your mental skills and working diligently at building up your confidence level.

How to Build More Leverage

Timing and deadlines, discussed in Chapter 10, can be used to your benefit if the other party is under strict company-imposed limitations or under contract to deliver goods and services at a specified date and time. If you have a concession that advantageously affects the other party's timeline, your offer is going to become very attractive.

Likewise, try to predict what issues your counterpart will be most interested in. A good place to start is at the heart of what all people in business focus on:

- Money
- Profitability
- Reputation
- Gain
- Loss

Look for concessions that fall into these categories, and use them to appeal to the other party's most imperative goals and his means of reaching them. If you sense he's taking advantage of your underdog position, remind him that you're well aware of the leverage you have by focusing his attention on how what you have to offer fits into the above points.

ALERT!

Sometimes the other party is overconfident and figures that since you're the underdog, you should easily give up your concessions to him. If you experience this situation, make it clear that you will not settle for an unsatisfactory agreement.

No matter how unpleasant the other party might be to work with, using status as an excuse to be rude, belittling, uncompromising, or impatient, don't cave in. If you do, you'll only confirm his assumptions about your weakness and the entire negotiation will go downhill from there. Instead, stand up for yourself and let it be known that you won't be steamrolled. Your counterpart will begin to take you more seriously and will have more respect for you in the long run.

Master Your Field

If lack of knowledge about the issues at hand makes you the underdog, take it upon yourself to bridge the gap. Attend a seminar or workshop that teaches negotiating skills. Take classes at your local college, and meet with specialists in the field to gain as much hands-on experience as possible. Become proactive by networking at the office and other appropriate meeting spots, and do something that gives you a little bit of recognition, like publishing an article in the newspaper.

All of these examples are immediate ways to compensate for some of the strengths you lack. Sure, it takes years to build a reputation, something you obviously can't do by the time you meet with your counterpart. However, get the ball rolling by making contact with your peers now. The information and advice you can get from them today could prove to be invaluable for the deals of tomorrow.

If You're Not Ready Yet

Simply put, if you're not ready to negotiate, don't do it. Maybe you need more time to prepare, or maybe you need more information from the other party; whatever the reason, do not put yourself in a position you'll regret later. Let your counterpart know you're not ready, and if he still persists on beginning the meeting, give him an exact date you'll be ready so he knows you're not purposely putting it off.

If you need additional information from the other party, ask them to provide this to you. Explain how these details, for example fixed percentage rates, will help you solve the conflict that's preventing you from beginning the negotiation process. Your counterpart should have no problem acquiescing to your request, and if he does, find out why. The answer you receive could be another important factor for you to consider before making your offer.

If you find yourself in a difficult situation (death in the family, illness), give yourself enough time to fully recover before you start making deals. You need to be clear-headed, focused, and reactive. That's hard to do if you can't stop crying or if you're incessantly coughing and sneezing. Your disposition will also distract the other party, and it could incite her to take advantage of you.

One Winner, One Loser

A win/lose outcome results when positional negotiating tactics dominate the majority of the bargaining process, whereby one person thinks she got the better deal over the other. This comes about because both parties have their feet firmly planted on either side of the fence, and neither one is willing to move. They act irrationally toward each other, using pride and arrogance to focus on their ultimate goal of satisfying the ego instead of focusing on a positive solution for both parties.

This behavior is catastrophic for business dealings because hardly anything good ever comes out of it, even for the person who thinks she's won. In retrospect, both parties will hopefully understand that nobody walked away feeling satisfied. Because they focused on maintaining their positions, they could not establish trust or communicate their goals and objectives. When winning becomes more important than finding the best solution, both parties will suffer. Frustration more than anything else will serve as the catalyst for making and agreeing to concessions, in which the competition becomes a game of "the more I get, the less I have to give."

When No One Wins

Also known as a lose/lose outcome, deadlock occurs when negotiations come to an impasse, in which both parties have used up all their concessions. Progress seems out of reach, and disappointment fills the room because it seems like no matter how many times you go over the issues, favorable solutions are nowhere in sight. Both parties lose because neither side accomplished the main goals they set out to achieve. Additionally, emotional responses to the stalemate could include anger and blame, and what follows is a collapse of communication.

FACT

The one good thing about deadlock is that it's not always permanent. There are ways to get around it if you stay calm and allow your mind to be open to a variety of different possibilities.

One of the main reasons for deadlock is that the best possible solution hasn't been discovered yet. If the other party is not playing fair and refuses to be more flexible than she's been, chances are there's something she's holding onto that could possibly breathe new life into the discussion and take it out of deadlock status. She may or may not know that she has this element, so it's up to you to try to get it out of her. Get everyone in the room to start brainstorming to warm up their creative-thinking skills.

Another way to try to get out of deadlock is to take a break by getting something to eat or drink or going for a walk. When everyone comes back, see what you can resolve with the smaller issues before you get back to the deadlock problem. It'll serve as a warm-up for when the larger issue does come up again.

Knowing When to Opt Out

Sometimes, no matter how much time you've invested into making a deal work, there comes a point where you realize you want to walk away. The reasons might be readily apparent—you're not satisfied with the final offer; you turned up information about the other party that makes you uncomfortable about entering into an agreement with her; one (or more) of your alternatives presented a better offer; or you want to take an extended period of time to do more research and seek out a better alternative (if you don't have one already).

FACT

Intuition, grossly undervalued by some people because of its subjective nature, plays a significant role in negotiation. People distrust intuition because they are unable to legitimize it with tangible evidence, and they aren't comfortable with relying on it. They can follow their hearts, but it's tougher for them to trust their instincts.

Other reasons are more psychological or intuitive. For example, if your counterpart has been quarrelsome, demanding, rude, and downright difficult to work with from the very beginning, you'll have to determine if this is the kind of person you have the patience and stamina to handle throughout the life of the contract, because it's likely his behavior will not improve in the long run. If problems arise in the future, he may prove to be just as ornery as he was throughout the negotiation period (if not more so).

The price you have to pay to settle a negotiation might not always be a harrowing experience, but it can be a financial burden. If you're not careful, you can end up doling out an exorbitant amount to attorneys and the like for fees, commissions, and anything else that might warrant a price tag. If the bill for these services is considerably more than the magnitude of your deal, consider bowing out gracefully.

If you've ever taken a wrong turn in a strange town and had the urge to lock your car doors without even thinking about it, you're listening to the instinctive part of yourself that feels threatened—without knowing why—and seeks safety. Even if you're not used to reacting on instinct alone, pay attention to any signs or "bad feelings" you experience during the meeting and investigate a little further. If the other party makes you uncomfortable for reasons you're not yet aware of, talk to the people he works with to see what you can learn. You might be surprised to discover how badly he treats his employees or how ruthless he is with his peers.

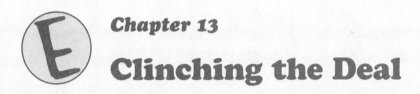

Chapter 13

Clinching the Deal

You're almost there! Exciting as that may sound, you still have a few more challenges to overcome. These trials will no doubt test your perseverance, determination, and skill, but they will also bring you closer to reaching a well-deserved closure and help you avoid roadblocks that can (and often do) prevent this agreement from happening.

Knowing What to Expect

When you're in the thick of a negotiation, it's easy to get caught up swapping concessions and making offers and counteroffers. You're trying to keep up with deciphering the other person's body language, mood, sincerity, and next move. You must constantly take stock of how much leverage you have, re-evaluate where you stand with your give-and-takes, and reaffirm that your goals are being met. Whew! No wonder you may forget there's an end in sight. It's a long, arduous road to travel, but the final destination is worth putting up with the occasional bump or two.

ALERT!

People have a tendency to panic when time is almost up, partly out of fear of losing your business, and partly out of fear they won't achieve their goals. As a result, deals of all sorts are put on the table in a desperate attempt to keep the negotiation moving. Avoid this trap. Otherwise, in a mad rush to the finish line, you won't think everything through and could end up giving too much away.

You can expect a lot to happen during the final stages of the negotiation. Consequently, you'll have to rely on your keen business sense to pick up on important clues that surface when closure is near. If you've been studying the steps in this book, you will have indeed been applying your new skills every step of the way and should be able to recognize the tactics you've learned as they appear. Although the knowledge you've acquired thus far can be applied at this stage, there are some additional techniques and points you'll want to know.

Keep It Separate from the Rest

Closing is one step in the process, and for that reason should be treated as a separate matter. It comes with its own set of obstacles you'll need to get around and involves a great deal of creative thinking. Regard it as a review of everything you and the other party have discussed. Some agreements could have been made so long ago (hours, days, months), they'll need to be reiterated and verified.

When you're ready to close, ask your counterpart if he agrees. If so, clearly state that everything you'll be discussing from here on out will be part of the closure. Some negotiators handle closing with a completely different mindset and a totally different approach, so give them the courtesy of preparing themselves for it instead of unexpectedly springing it on them.

Working Through Objections

Since closure requires the go-ahead from both parties, problems could arise if one party objects to one or more of the terms. In this case, you'll have to use your best negotiating skills to work through the objections and preclude deadlock. As frustrating as it might be, don't lose your cool by displaying aggressive or condescending behavior. You're close to the end—the last thing you want to do is jeopardize the relationship and hinder clear decision-making. Acknowledge that the disagreements are sound, even if you don't think they are; your counterpart is more likely to treat you with the same courtesy. Work with the other party, not against her, to pinpoint where the problems lie.

If you sense there's a deeper issue than your counterpart is willing to admit, try to coax it out of her by asking questions such as, "It seems like you're feeling something isn't quite right at this point—is their another issue that concerns you?" Be empathetic, and offer to help the other person if she needs it.

Make sure every issue is dealt with right then and there. Otherwise, it's sure to come up again later and it will be harder to resolve because you'll be even deeper into the arrangement.

When and How to Close

Though you should always be looking for opportunities to close, there are some obvious and some not-so-obvious signals that let you know when the moment is right to make this vital move. If all parties feels that their objectives have been achieved and their main goals have been satisfied, then you're ready to move on.

Similarly, if there's a solution readily available to one of the main issues you've been struggling with and both parties are in agreement, sound the horns, blow the whistles, and get the wheels rollin'—you're ready to go! Another common reason for closing is a pressing deadline. Above all, if you and the other party should feel that you have settled on enough of the issues, you're ready to map out the details and close the deal.

At this point, you're probably eager to make it official—but hold on. There's one thing you need to do before concluding the negotiation period. Allow time for you and your counterpart to go over the notes you made throughout the course of the discussion. On a separate sheet of paper, outline all the agreements that were made and the details and terms that were discussed. List your concessions, the other party's concessions, concessions that were grouped together, and any contingencies that were made regarding these decisions. Write everything as clearly and thoroughly as you understand it to be. If everything goes smoothly, these will be the conditions of your contract.

FACT

From a legal standpoint, closure occurs when all the agreed-upon details are finalized into a legally binding signed contract, witnessed and verified by all parties. Read the entire contract, and sign when you're ready. Take your time and feel good about what you've accomplished!

Next, compare your notes with those of your counterpart, or if he didn't take notes, read each item on your list out loud. The point of this exercise is to be sure that both you and the other party understand the agreement in the same way. If you thought he was paying the shipping charges in exchange for a 20-percent discount on production fees but he thought he was paying 20-percent of the shipping, you'll want to work that out.

Last-Minute Concessions

When things aren't going as smoothly as you hoped, and the other party is still unable to accept the conditions as they stand, offer a concession. Not a big one, but one that is worth something to them. This gesture shows the other person that you're truly giving it your best shot to make the deal work for both of you. Each of you has invested a lot of time and energy into coming up with the best deal that's in you to create; there's no reason someone should be shortchanged. If giving up a minor concession means something major to your counterpart and to the deal as a whole, go for it. Wouldn't you feel better walking away from the table together to celebrate a mutual achievement, instead of gloating alone about a victory? Herein lies the beauty of win/win negotiating.

What's Stopping You?

As strange as it sounds, some people never want to reach the end of a negotiation. They might experience more anxiety at the closing stage than during the bargaining stage. It's a big step, not to mention a major commitment.

Remember that feeling you had when you bought your first car? First computer? First home? After spending months researching, comparing, and reworking your budget to make the best possible purchase, you reach that part of the transaction when you're just about ready to make your dream a reality. You're excited, nervous, pensive, happy, and unsure all at once. So how are you ever going to make it through the closing with that mindset? Stop for a moment to think about how you feel and why you feel that way. Once you determine the cause of your anguish, you'll feel better about completing the deal.

Overcoming Fear

Negotiating may seem intimidating at first, but once you get going, you feel more comfortable. During the negotiation process, you experience many emotions and you learn how to work through them as you resolve the issues under discussion. But when closing time nears, those old feelings seem to return to the forefront. The closing is your final step—you don't get to come back to the table tomorrow to hash out the details again. That in itself is enough to scare anyone off! If you've been prepared the entire time, covered all your major points, and feel good about how the other party fared, then you've done your job and deserve to give yourself (and your counterpart) the opportunity to close the deal, write it down, and make it official.

If the fear won't subside, ask yourself what is making you nervous. Do you still feel uneasy about a particular issue? Are there any unanswered questions you have about a deadline? Try to determine what might be causing you to fear the end of the meeting. It's natural to feel anxious, but fight it with everything you've got and keep going.

QUESTION?

How do I know if fear and not dissatisfaction is preventing me from closing the deal?
Take a break and go over everything with a colleague or friend. Review your goals and ask yourself if they've been met; seek positive reinforcement in the objectives you completed. Continue to survey the facts and if you feel good about them, it's safe to assume your reluctance is originating from the grips of fear.

Controlling Doubt

While questions about details like price, discounts, and deadlines are often easily answered, intangible questions that point to uncertainty and doubt can prevent you from making the commitment. You might wonder if there's more you could've done or if you should've fought harder for a particular issue; insecurity can have you wondering if you were a pushover or if you held your own; panic can make you feel like you've forgotten something or that you're just not ready to close.

All of these mental blocks will cause you to second-guess yourself and lose faith in a deal you felt good about closing just five minutes ago. Don't let your confidence be shattered with your own doubt. It's okay to feel apprehensive, but take control of it before it ruins what you've worked so hard to achieve.

Moreover, by dragging your feet, you run the risk of losing your counterpart's respect and possibly the deal. He might lose his patience or begin to have questions of his own, and the last thing you want to do is give him time to second-guess himself too. Have faith in yourself, your work, and the negotiation, and close the deal knowing you did the best you could possibly do. The key to successful negotiating isn't about how many times you can win the game. It's about careful planning, honest problem-solving, and sharp instincts—all of which help you achieve the goals you set out to accomplish.

Extras and Perks

If you're ready to close but the other party is still ambivalent, there are a few things you can do to help ease them into closure. In addition to helping you bring your negotiation to a successful conclusion, extras and perks can help you show that you have character and an excellent business sense.

As stated previously, you should always be trying to develop a good relationship with your counterpart, whether you're verifying information with them during the preparation stage, bargaining with them during the negotiating stage, or composing the contract together. The relationships you begin building today will over time blossom into great friendships and successful partnerships that both of you continuously benefit from. There may be other opportunities for you to work together. By establishing good business practices now, you're ensuring favorable results for the future.

Be Reassuring

A little enthusiasm goes a long way, especially when your counterpart shows hesitation. Just a few encouraging words may be just what she needs to hear to move on. You can also point out all the objectives the other party has accomplished. Sometimes hearing them listed out loud makes a bigger impact than just quietly thinking them over. Go over any deadlines that were agreed on. Say something like, "By June 1st, you'll have the first shipment so you'll be able to ship to your customers way ahead of schedule." This will help the other party get a clear picture of how she benefits from the transactions that took place. Positive energy is contagious, so use it often.

Be Considerate

As part of your planning, compile a list of several small concessions that you wouldn't mind giving up, if needed. Use them as backup for when you need to apply a little push. Your counterpart will certainly appreciate the favor, and hopefully that will be all she needs to overcome last-minute indecision.

ALERT!

While it's good to have something in reserve for emergencies, be careful you don't give too much away. Once you've agreed to close, leave it at that. Don't try to rehash issues you've already agreed on—you could be opening up a can of worms. At this point in the game, you want to reassure, review, and revise if necessary, but you definitely don't want to renegotiate.

The Key to Success

The key to a successful close is thinking about it from day one. Everything you do—research, planning, bargaining, relationship building—should be done with closing in mind. When doing research, think about what you can use as last-minute concessions; when planning, have backups set in place at every stage of the game, and come up with answers to "what if" questions; while bargaining, continue to move forward and take steps to avoid an impasse; and whenever possible, create a positive atmosphere and establish trust and respect by showing goodwill. You want to satisfy your goals. However, the overall goal is to get to the close and make everything official.

Remember, closing is a separate step that requires as much diligence as all the other steps did. You should never rush through it. Here are the closing checkpoints you need to be sure you follow through with:

- ☐ First, confirm that everyone is in agreement, making sure everything has been worked out and there's nothing left to close. Use the list of concessions you made to once again verify all terms and conditions, if needed.
- ☐ Next, review the agenda to be sure everything has been covered and all major points have been discussed.
- ☐ Finally, create a few to-do lists, recording deadlines to follow up on and deadlines to meet.

The Moment of Glory

Congratulations! The closing is finished, and it's time to sign the contracts. Grab your finest champagne glasses along with your favorite ballpoint pen and make a toast to yourself, your counterpart, and the success of your negotiation! Reward yourself for all your hard work—go out for dinner, throw yourself a party, celebrate! You've certainly earned it.

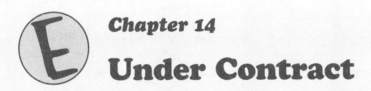

Chapter 14

Under Contract

Although the details of a contract are not fleshed out until the end of a meeting, it's important to keep them in mind throughout the entire negotiation period. Taking good notes and writing down everything that's agreed upon will not only ensure you include everything you want in the contract, but it will also help clear up the hazy points that were discussed hours or even days beforehand.

Contracts Galore

Contracts serve to record agreements that two or more parties have made with each other and to outline the stipulations of those agreements. A good contract should protect the investments of the parties involved. Contracts are legal documents and hold up in court. There are literally thousands of different types of contracts, ranging from a template contract you find online to a specific contract written up following negotiations.

Form Contracts

Form or boilerplate contracts are templates that represent the bare bones of a company's demands. Most real estate agencies and mortgage brokers will use the same form contract for every client, listing the conditions, limitations, and delivery expectations the company demands, amending the boilerplate only to reflect the terms and provisions unique to each situation. The set-in-stone appearance of this type of contract may seem intimidating, so it's important to keep in mind that form contracts really aren't indisputable—any part can be changed. Read these contracts carefully and thoroughly, and don't skip any sections. Mark any changes you have right on the contract, and initial the changes.

FACT

Boilerplates are often riddled with convoluted statements and words, such as "heretofore," "hereinafter," "thereof," "thereto," "hereof," and "in furtherance of." When you come across this type of legalese in your contract, ask for an explanation. Don't be embarrassed—*no one* (except lawyers) knows what this stuff means. Also, get the translations for any Latin phrase, like "arguendo", "ab initio," "ad rem," and "haec verba."

Drafting a Contract

You may draft your own contract or have a professional draft it for you. If the latter is the case, you want to keep several points in mind. First, decide who will be the one to draw up the contract, and make sure everyone agrees whom that person will be. Next, start with a basic contract and work from there. You can either download one from the Internet or acquire one from an attorney or other legal official. Appendix A includes a list of Web sites that offer printable contracts. Generic forms are free, such as living wills and demand for payment letters, but the more complex forms like negotiating forms come with hefty price tags. Some Web sites also allow you to view sample contracts like those used for business mergers.

Note Taking

However you and the other party choose to have the contract drawn, you should always be thinking about what information you want to be clearly stated on the form. Taking notes from the beginning of the discussion right up until the signing of the contract prevents crucial details such as the following from being left out, muddled, misconstrued, or denied:

- Your and the other party's gains—big and small
- Conditions on which these gains are based
- Referenced material, such as price lists, warranty information, or insurance policies
- Any emotional clues you picked up from the other party (especially helpful in assessing the party's sincerity and comfort level to estimate whether they'll be able to make good on a particular obligation)
- Important deadlines—both yours and the other party's
- Anything and everything pertinent to the courses of action agreed upon

A note about note-taking: review them carefully, especially if someone else has rewritten them for you. There's always a chance one of your points was misinterpreted or left out.

Don't forget to jot down notes after each phone call, e-mail, and other communication. Also mark the date and time the initial contact took place so any changes that were discussed are on record. If not written down immediately, these things are easy to forget, especially if you're involved in a month-long negotiation process.

In Charge of Writing

After you decide what kind of contract you want to use, you'll need to agree on who will be in charge of writing it. If you've been faithfully taking notes, it might already be assumed that you're the one spearheading the negotiation and should therefore be in charge of drafting the contract. This could be of great advantage to you, but do not assume the role if you are not ready for it.

Benefits of Being the Contractor

In his book, *The Negotiation Toolkit: How to Get Exactly What You Want in Any Business or Personal Situation,* Roger J. Volkema argues that offering to write up the agreement benefits you in two ways. First, it relieves the other party of the dreadful task and is usually interpreted as a rather generous offer. Second, once you're crowned "Contractor," you have full reign over what is included into the document, including terms, conditions, and the specific language used.

Once you've written up the contract, have a lawyer look it over. Most lawyers charge only a small fee, and their expertise is invaluable. They can provide insight into issues you weren't aware of and correct any mistakes.

Volkema goes on to suggest that writing up the other party's compensations first reassures them that you have their best interests in mind and that you aren't just focusing on making sure all of your points are included. If one of your goals is to build a strong business relationship with the other party, then it might be in your best interest to volunteer to write the contract so as to give the other person a glimpse into your honorable character and help build confidence in your business practices.

Third-Party Contractors

If all parties involved choose not to write the contract, a third party will be called in to draw it up and to oversee all changes, questions, and issues. This third party person can be a lawyer or business partner and should be impartial. She should be there from the very beginning of the negotiation to take notes, writing down all the important factors stated in the previous section of this chapter.

Hammering Out the Details

Putting together a contract is almost as fun as writing user manuals. The details are so minute that it's easy to zone out and overlook a few. There are some checkpoints you can put into place that will help you identify gaps as well as help you know what important information should be included.

Terms of Agreement

Everything that was agreed upon, including the conditions that were placed on those agreements, should be written into the contract. This includes but is not limited to deadlines, obligations, and consequences of termination. All specific details should be clearly written out. Say what you mean, and mean what you say. If you enter into a contract to have your dining room painted and you expect the painter to remove the wallpaper first, make that point clear in the contract. If you want the painter to blend three particular shades of green to use as the primary color on the walls, include that statement as well. Details, details, and more details are what should be included in this section of the contract. Knowing what to expect and knowing what's expected of you reduces the likelihood of disputes later on.

Unpredictable Circumstances

Make sure you and the other party knows full well what the outcome will be if something unexpected happens. If there's a fire and the dining room is damaged before the painter has completed it, who will be responsible for payment? Will the contract become null and void?

Always make sure there are alternative solutions set in place. Try to imagine every possible scenario (relative to the agreement) and devise solutions that will be immediately put into action if one of the scenarios takes place. Expect the unexpected, and you'll never be left in the dark about how to handle the "what ifs."

Consequences of Breaching

Have a clause worked into the contract that states what the consequences will be if either party fails to uphold the contract. Be advised that some people enter into negotiations with every intention of breaching the contract. If a party has breached the contract, sending a notice of protest to the damaging party preserves your rights and serves as proof in a court of law that a breach has manifested.

QUESTION?

What does "failure of consideration" mean?
Failure of consideration is essentially the same as breaching a contract. It literally means you didn't hold up your part of the bargain. At this point, the contract becomes null and void, and the person who has been wronged can withhold making good on her considerations and/ or take legal action against the other party.

In Consideration

Consideration is basically a fancy term for benefits, gains, or promises. According to *www.nolo.com*, a Web site that translates the language of law into language the rest of us can understand, a contract is only legal and valid if something of value is exchanged for something else of value, and both parties must agree on all the terms. Even further, some states require that these considerations need to be in writing in order for the contract to be considered a legal document.

Reviewing the Contract

When the time comes for you to look over the contract, you'll need to pay attention. Read every word of every page, and check all the factual information (particularly the spelling of your name and the dates) for accuracy. Double-check to make sure that all agreed-upon gains for both sides are listed. If there's anything that you don't understand or that doesn't make sense, ask for clarification. Use common sense—if the contract is too complicated, get professional help in reviewing it. If something needs to be changed, have both parties initial all changes. Sign every page, and insist on an original copy if one isn't provided to you.

Understand What You Read

Surely the most frustrating part about reading a contract is knowing how to translate all the mumbo jumbo. But you shouldn't be intimidated by legalese or let it prevent you from asking questions about anything you don't understand. Neglecting to ask for clarification of certain terms and statements could end up hurting you in the future. If something doesn't make sense, ask for an explanation; if it still doesn't make sense, ask again or ask someone else.

Do's and Don'ts

Following a few do's and don'ts helps you evaluate your contract and points out what should be double-checked. Use this list as a starting point to make sure you've covered your bases:

- Do crosscheck all documents and paperwork referred to in the contract.
- Do check for amendments the other party made—you'll need to initial these.

- Do make sure the other party has agreed to and signed your amendments—as much as you don't want any surprises, neither does anyone else.
- Do read the fine print.
- Do read all boilerplate material.
- Don't skip over sections because they look too exhausting to read.
- Don't forget to check the numbers—dates, prices, discounts, fees, and compensation.
- Don't assume that everything is correct.

Rework the contract as many times as you need to until you're completely satisfied. Keep in mind that while it's okay to rework the contract, you shouldn't overwork it—you don't want to renegotiate everything if it's not necessary.

Meeting of Minds

When the final contract has been drawn and all amendments have been reflected, there should be one final sit-down meeting with you, the other party, and the person who drafted the contract. If you've hired a lawyer to look over the contract, or if you've been consulting with your business partner, it's not a bad idea to have them attend and witness the final signing.

Reading and signing the contract together ensures everyone is on the same page and generates a comfortable atmosphere for taking the time to read every word. Again, don't feel rushed, and don't feel that it's ever too late to make more changes. Once everything is signed, feel free to jump up and down with glee that the negotiation is done.

Take your time, and don't feel pressured into signing the contract right away. On the other hand, if the other party is taking days to look over the contract and claiming the need to have his business partners, lawyers, and everyone under the sun look it over, set a time limit that makes the contract void if it's not signed by the specified date and time.

Reciprocal Promises

Throughout the course of a negotiation, many promises are made, usually with good intentions. But after the agreements have been put in writing, and everyone has signed their lives away on the dotted line, there's no telling where the deal will go from the there. To keep everybody honest, monitor progress, be aware of approaching deadlines, and don't be afraid to contact the other party with concerns or possibly damaging developments. Creating a spreadsheet in Microsoft Excel or a similar software program to highlight deadlines, goals, and obligations will help you stay on top of things and avoid being surprised by a fast-approaching deadline you thought was further away than it actually was.

Take every promise you made seriously, and consistently deliver each time. Be the better businessperson, and show the other party you are just as interested in his goals and objectives as you are about yours. More often than not, he will feel the same as you do, which will make it a pleasure for both of you to do business with each other in the future.

If the other party is someone who fails to live up to his part of the deal, remind him of the contract you both signed, and be prepared to seek litigation if he continues to ignore your requests for action.

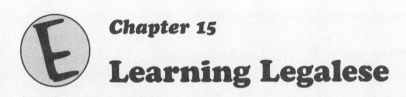

Chapter 15

Learning Legalese

It's important to get the details of a contract settled in order to help prevent problems from arising in the future. But what about the things you cannot control, such as unpredictable circumstances or breaches? If the other party has broken an agreement that was under contract, the legal system has your back. This chapter talks about the laws that protect you, the laws that bind you, and the processes that are involved in both.

Contract Law

A lot can happen between the time you sign the contract and the time it ends. Problems could arise that put either you or the other party in danger of being unable to fulfill your obligations, and you'll need to know the best way to handle those situations. For instance, if you contracted a painter to paint your dining room in a specified amount of time and he didn't show up on the last day to complete the job, how long should you wait before contacting a lawyer? Are you entitled to compensation if you entered into an agreement with a person whose nonperformance cost you money?

Contract law answers these and other questions about your rights as party to a contract. It represents all parties who are responsible for meeting the terms as specified in the contract they signed.

FACT

While a simple handshake can close the deal, it's not always enforceable by law. The best way to protect yourself is to get the agreement in writing—especially if it contains a long list of concessions that were made and accepted by you and the other party. If you don't put everything in writing, you'll have a hard time trying to prove to a judge that the other party didn't do what he said he would.

Contract law holds parties accountable for neglecting to satisfy their part of the deal. Let's say you and another person agree that in one week, you will buy his car for $5,000. You explain that you'll need to sell the car you currently own in order to get the $5,000. After the week is up and your car is sold, you go back to the car owner only to discover he's already sold the car to someone else for $6,000.

Though a written contract may not exist, a verbal promise was made in which you and the other party agreed to the details that were specified. You made plans based on that agreement, and contract law protects your right to perform acts that are contingent on those promises. It holds the other party responsible for failing to make good on his promise. Of course, if you have a written contract, your chances of proving your case are significantly greater.

Withdrawing from the Contract

Most of us have experienced buyer's remorse at one point. You find something you like, buy it, then change your mind and decide you no longer want it. Usually, you can return the item to the store and get a refund, but it works differently with items that can't easily be returned, such as a house or a car.

When you enter into a business contract, a lot depends on what the other party is willing do to. If you want to get out of the contract, the other party might simply allow it in order to maintain the integrity of the relationship. Maybe there was an oversight on your part, such as an accounting error that won't allow you to live up to your promises, or maybe something unexpected happened and your counterpart feels cutting you loose is the better choice. She also might have the foresight to know that if she doesn't let you out of the contract now, it may be difficult for you to live up to your side of the contract, thus making it more difficult for her to operate her business.

Though your counterpart may be empathetic with your reasons for wanting to cancel the contract, she's not obliged to let you do it. If she decides not to let you out of the contract, you'll have to hire a lawyer to discuss your options.

If your counterpart wants to cancel the contract, use your judgment to decide if it's in your best interest to excuse her.

QUESTION?

What is a release?

A release is when you relinquish claims, actions, and/or any rights against another party, freeing them of any responsibilities that were either stated in the original contract or were a result of something. For example, if you borrow someone's car for two days and sign a release that states you're not responsible for any engine damage that appears during that time period, the owner cannot sue you or expect you to pay for the repairs.

The FTC's Cooling-Off Rule

The Federal Trade Commission (FTC) states that if you purchase an item of $25 or more outside of the retailer's permanent address and you change your mind about the transaction, you're entitled to a full refund within three days of the date of purchase. The rule applies to any sales that were made from your home, office, or dormitory, as well as hotel rooms and restaurants.

The following is a list of exceptions to the rule as posted on the FTC's Web site, *www.ftc.gov*. The cooling-off rule does not cover the following kinds of sales:

- Those under $25
- Those for goods or services not primarily intended for personal, family, or household purposes (the rule does apply to courses of instruction or training)
- Those made entirely by mail or telephone
- Those that are the result of prior negotiations at the seller's permanent business location where the goods are sold regularly
- Those needed to meet an emergency
- Those made as part of your request for the seller to do repairs or maintenance on your personal property (purchases made beyond the maintenance or repair request are covered)

ALERT!

If a salesperson comes to your home and sells you a vacuum cleaner, the cooling-off rule is in effect for that sale. The seller must also inform you of your right to cancel the order and the steps that need to be taken to do so.

Other exempt items include real estate, insurance, or securities; automobiles, vans, trucks, or other motor vehicles sold at temporary locations, provided the seller has at least one permanent place of business; and arts or crafts sold at fairs or locations such as shopping malls, civic centers, and schools.

Visit the FTC Web site for complete guidelines on how to cancel your purchase using the cooling-off rule. You can also reach the FTC by telephone at ☎1-877-FTC-HELP (☎1-877-382-4357).

One-Sided Contracts

It's important that you know exactly what you're getting in a negotiation and in the written contract. You don't want to get stuck with a deal that you later realize is unfair. The judge will not excuse you from a contract on the grounds that it's a bad deal. If you buy a computer for $7,000 only to find out later that it's worth $2,000, you'll have to live with the loss.

That's why research and preparation are essential, not only when you're negotiating with large corporations or small business, but when you're entering into an agreement as a customer as well. Clearly, in the case of the computer purchase, not enough comparison shopping was done. No matter what you're negotiating, look at the competition. Compare price, quantity, timeline, quality, availability, and so on. Be sure that what you're getting meets your standards as compared to those of the rest of the world. If you're buying new computers for your employees, confirm that they will come with the most updated software.

While you cannot be exonerated from poor business arrangements, judges will in certain cases annul an illegal contract. For example, if a sixteen-year old signs a contract to buy a laptop computer, the contract is not binding because he is a minor and needs parental consent to sign it. If the store doesn't usually allow returns on laptops, they will have to in this case because the contract was unlawful.

When you buy something at the store, your receipt is your contract. It states the time and date you made the purchases, what items were purchased, how much they cost (including tax), and the form of payment you used. Some receipts print the establishment's return policy on either the front or the back so you can't dispute their procedures.

Breach of Contract

A breach transpires when one party fails to perform what the contract states he has agreed to do. It occurs when the other party cannot perform her own duties; when the offending party does something that goes against what the contract states; or when the offending party simply will not do what's expected of her. You'll have to decide how severe the breach is before you decide to handle the matter in court.

For example, if your counterpart delivered goods three days past the agreed-upon ship date but the late shipment didn't harm your business, you might let it slide this time, discuss it with her to prevent it from happening again, and be on the lookout for any breaches that occur in the future. If, however, you decide that the breach is too significant to ignore, there are many options available to you.

Specific Performance

In a court of law, the defendant may be ordered "specific performance"— to complete the terms of the contract rather than or in addition to paying damages. Note that this form of ruling is rarely made. It is reserved primarily for real estate cases in which the seller changes his mind and doesn't want to go through with the promise he made to the buyer. If it is granted, the offending party will have to deliver the goods, perform the job and/or make the payment required of him in the contract.

One of the reasons specific performance is regarded as a privilege rather than a useful solution is that it's difficult to monitor. It would be timely and costly for the court to oversee every action that a judge ordered someone to do. Also, if left to the discretion of the injured party, people would be running in and out of court to complain about how the other party didn't do the job right. For example, if you brought your car in to be detailed and it came back looking dirty, and the judge awarded specific performance of the car to be detailed again, how would he determine if the job was ever done? To make matters worse, if you went into court to complain about a speck of dirt on the console, how would the judge know you're not overreacting?

Usually in cases like this one, the court will reward a justifiable dollar amount that allows the injured party to get the services performed again by someone else. It actually makes more sense to do it this way because it might be difficult to place your trust in the person who breached the contract to do a good job the second time around.

Resolution Options

There are many ways to get what was promised you and most of them, not surprisingly, involve money. In addition to assessing the value of your losses, the judge might require the other party to pay any attorney fees that accrued from the time the contract was breached. He might also order the other party to pay "consequential and incidental damages," money awarded for losses that were predicted if a breach occurred. Going back to the car-sale example, since the car owner knew you were selling your old car in order to pay for the car he was selling you, and he sold the car to someone else anyway, he'll be required to pay these damages because he was aware of the contingency.

QUESTION?

What is a tort?
A tort is similar to a breach of contract, but it usually involves some sort of intentional physical action, such as a punch in the face or a kick in the stomach or an unintentional act, like accidentally knocking someone over with a bicycle. It's a civil wrongdoing that requires a remedy from the court.

Other remedies pertain to the state of the contract itself. If the judge decides on a "rescission" of the contract, the contract is canceled, all advancements are to be paid back, and all parties are no longer responsible for their portion of the terms.

Good Faith or Bad Faith?

When two or more parties enter into a negotiation, it is under the assumption that all parties involved will be honorable and live up to their contractual commitments. Good faith also implies that everyone will be fair and truthful in order to satisfy the purpose of the initial meeting. When a party makes concessions she has no intention of fulfilling, she is acting in bad faith because she is deceptively giving the impression she is serious about the negotiation. Though there is no way to tell if someone is acting in good or bad faith, some signs to watch out for may include extraneous delays, unnecessary postponements, and refusal to make concessions on major issues. Good faith and bad faith practices get a little more involved when dealing with real estate and insurance, which we'll discuss later in this book.

Misrepresentation and Duress

If the other party tells you something that he knows is false, and you sign the contract based on your belief of that statement to be true, you can have the contract rescinded in court. The same holds true even if the other party was unaware that the information was false. Keep in mind that if you have the contract cancelled, you'll be required to give back any benefits you received. This includes money, products, keys to the company car, and warranties, to name a few.

A similar circumstance involves signing a contract under duress. If you were drugged, held at gunpoint, or threatened in any way that made you sign against your will, the contract is not considered to be a legal document. A contract can only be valid if both parties willfully agree to its terms. It cannot be enforced if one party is made to do something he would not have done under ordinary conditions.

Fraud

According to the *Merriam-Webster's Dictionary of Law,* the legal definition of fraud is "an intentional perversion of truth for the purpose of obtaining some valuable thing or promise from another." Similar to misrepresentation, fraud is an act in which a person presents false information, causing a counterpart to suffer one or many losses. The difference is that fraud is always intentional.

Fraud rears its ugly head in many situations, from social security claims to insurance policies. There are many laws and rules pertaining to this crime, including insider trading, which involves selling or purchasing securities (or stock) based on information that has not yet been made available to the general public. It's a criminal offense that is punished severely. You should examine your actions carefully if you're unsure whether you're in danger of committing the act.

Litigation As an Option

In its simplest form, litigation is the process of taking part in legal proceedings to solve a dispute; filing a lawsuit is engaging in litigation. There are many reasons why litigations come about—to decide who gets what in a divorce; to settle a malpractice suit; to determine who is in the wrong in an auto accident; to get someone to carry out their duties as stated in a mutual agreement, and so on. Anyone can file the claim—a small business, a large corporation, neighbors, coworkers, or governments—as long as they have an issue that they believe needs to be settled by the court system.

Not all lawsuits require an exorbitant amount of money, nor do they all take years to settle. However, they can get quite messy and complicated, especially when the parties involved cannot communicate in a civil manner, as happens all too often in a divorce. When this is the case, it gets harder to find a solution and it takes longer to work out the details of the settlement.

ALERT!

Lawyers and courts have all kinds of fees, so if you can settle the agreement amicably and quickly, it would be in your best interest to do so. Though there are some cases that are better left up to a judge to decide on, most disputes can be cleared up before ever going before the judge.

Filing a lawsuit shouldn't be a decision that's made in haste. Retain a lawyer to determine the best possible way to resolve your issue. While she may or may not suggest litigation, her advice is invaluable. If your decision is to sue, your lawyer will be able to tell you how much time you have to file the claim, depending on the laws in your state. She will also take you through the many steps that are required, including the pre-litigation settlement discussion—a discussion which gives you and the other party another chance to reach an agreement before going to court. If a resolution cannot be made, the suit is filed and the other party responds by acknowledging that he is being sued.

Next, both parties and their lawyers will sit with the judge to discuss the basic elements of the lawsuit in a final effort to solve the issue outside of court. If this attempt fails, then a trial will be the next step, where a judgment is awarded.

Even if you've already filed a lawsuit, you can still settle the dispute on your own; once you settle, the suit will be dismissed. However, always consult a lawyer before making such a critical decision—once the suit is dismissed, it cannot be re-filed. Don't let inexperience guide you in the wrong direction.

Alternative Dispute Resolutions

Another function of contract law is to provide methods for resolving disputes outside of court. While your first response might be to sue the car owner for everything he's got because he left you without a car to get to work, it's best to find an alternative solution. A lawsuit can be lengthy, distressing, and expensive, and the longer it drags on, the longer you'll have to wait to get results.

Alternative dispute resolutions help you reach a solution faster than a lawsuit would, and there are three methods available:

- Negotiation and settlement
- Mediation
- Arbitration

The first one involves a process in which the parties discuss their dispute and hopefully reach a settlement. The last two methods involve a third party, and are discussed in the following sections.

Mediation

Mediation is a course of action that involves the intervention of a third party, a mediator. While the mediator can be someone who is highly knowledgeable in the issues being negotiated or mediated, the expertise isn't really necessary. Your mediator should be an expert in dispute resolution because her job is to help the disputing parties find some way to reach an agreement, especially when the negotiation is in deadlock.

The mediator offers a fresh perspective on the situation, which allows her to find the solution. Because she's working for both parties, she doesn't have a strong desire to hold onto certain concessions or make demands. Instead, the position she holds is to find the best possible outcome based on the facts and objectives of the concerned parties.

Mediation is not a legal proceeding, such as a trial, and the mediator cannot decide on what the parties have to agree to. It's a casual meeting in which the mediator talks to both parties together and then separately to help them refocus their attentions on their goals and what they're willing to do to reach them. Sometimes it's easy to lose sight of the purpose of the negotiation, and that's where a mediator can help.

Mediators are brought into negotiations and disputes to avoid litigation, although if a lawsuit has already been filed, they might be brought in to avoid accruing more lawyer and court costs. Since all parties involved share the mediator's fees, it's often the most favorable choice when considered from a financial standpoint.

Just like the contract that results from a negotiation, the agreement is documented, signed, and enforceable by law. If the agreement is reached after a lawsuit has been filed, the court will receive a copy, and the case will be dismissed.

Arbitration

Arbitration is similar to mediation in that it is a type of alternative dispute resolution that involves the inclusion of an outside party to help settle the dispute. What makes this process different is that the arbitrator directs a hearing and then decides who gets what. It's almost like litigation but is faster, cheaper, and more flexible. You don't have to worry about the court date's being pushed back because other cases take precedence over yours, and the parties can decide on the rules that will be in effect throughout the arbitration period.

For example, evidence that otherwise might not be allowed in court can be submitted in arbitration. Moreover, the parties can decide on who the arbitrators will be and whether the arbitration will be binding (parties must follow the arbitrator's final decisions) or nonbinding (parties take the award under advice and do not have to carry out the final decisions). Once the arbitration is finished, the resulting decision cannot be appealed. The conflict is considered resolved, and the case is closed.

FACT

Anyone can be an arbitrator, as long as both parties agree. Typically, arbitrators are experts on the subject that is being discussed, trusted community members (such as spiritual leaders), or those who have many years of experience in law (such as retired judges or lawyers).

When choosing an arbitrator, look for someone who is adept in managing arbitration hearings. Your candidate should have good written, oral, and organizational skills as well as the ability to summarize information quickly and make intelligent decisions.

Chapter 16

Building Confidence and Skills

Who says you have to be a professional guru in order to be a skilled negotiator? You are surrounded by an abundance of situations with opportunities that allow you to practice your skills; your entire world is your negotiating playground. There is a deal just waiting to be made in every store, eatery, service center, sales office, and home that you encounter. Everything truly is negotiable, and if it isn't, it doesn't hurt to ask. Use this chapter as your personal guide for finding ways to put your abilities to the test.

According to Script

One way to improve your negotiating skills is to create a script. You can write down what you plan to say and then create a hypothetical situation in which you get to act out your part of negotiations. Practicing like this will give you a better idea of how you will react in certain situations. You might even discover the hidden movie star in you! To get the full effect, solicit help from another person, choosing someone who makes you feel relaxed and secure.

It's important to practice with a person you're comfortable with. That's because the purpose of the exercise is to develop confidence by reacting naturally while you're at your best. If you're too busy worrying about what the other person thinks of you, you'll have a hard time recognizing what it feels like to be at ease with yourself during the negotiation.

Make a Speech

A great way to deliver your opening proposal is to write a speech. Studying the basics of how to go about it will prove to be invaluable in any situation that requires you to do a lot of talking. For more information on speech writing, visit *www.public-speaking.org* or *www.speechtips.com*. The first of those two Web sites includes a bunch of articles on various subjects, including how to get (and keep) the audience's attention. The second site is full of helpful tidbits, like what words to use to spice up your presentation.

First, deliver your speech separately to a few different people so you get a variety of responses. Choose people with diverse personalities so you can take notes on how different personality types react. Next, ask each person what he or she remembers about the speech. What words, issues, or actions did your audience find memorable? Finally, choose the responses from the person who resembles your negotiating counterpart the most. Tailor your speech to match the person's attention span and level of excitement about particular issues. If your target audience had a hard time staying focused on what you were saying, make your speech more interesting by using voice inflection, emphasis on words, and visual aids like slides or handouts.

FACT

Videotaping or recording yourself as you give the speech is the most effective way to keep track of your progress. Identify "filler" words that are used to replace uncomfortable silences. Watch out for "like," "you know," and "so," as well as murmurings like "um" and "ah." You'll want to correct these habits if you want the other party to feel that you're confident, intelligent, and prepared.

Role-Playing

You can have a lot of fun with this one. Not only does it provide great entertainment for family and friends, it also teaches you how to lighten up the mood when things get too serious for too long. Tension breeds more tension, and a few playful words or a tasteful joke can break the strenuous cycle. Of course, you'll need to think about whether your counterpart is receptive to comic relief.

Another benefit of role-playing is that it helps you remember things better. When you act out various scenes, you can get really creative when playing up the drama of the situation. Start off by having another person play the role of your counterpart. Let your helper choose a negotiating role to play (such as intimidator, seducer, or arguer) without telling you what it is. See if you can figure out what negotiating style the person is using and adjust your style as needed. Work through each of the styles outlined in Chapters 4 and 5 and have the person you're working with use all the tactics that were discussed in this book.

Take all the information you've gathered about your counterpart, his company, and his goals and use it to employ the tactics you're most worried about having to counter. It will be interesting to see how your helper reacts to them, especially if he or she devises new ways of handling each ploy.

You can also try switching roles to get a feel for how your counterpart will be defending each of his own points and to try to predict what kinds of concessions he'll be asking for. Additionally, this drill gives you a better understanding of his position as you walk in his shoes for a while.

The Devil's Advocate

Using this training technique helps you hone your skills by testing your own arguments and strategies. The person you choose to play devil's advocate will systematically reject everything you throw his way just for the sake of doing it. His job is to point out everything that could go wrong with either the negotiation or with the issues you bring up. If you use him to critique your negotiating strategy, he'll be asking you a lot of "what if" questions: What if the other party says this? What if your tactic backfires? What if you make a mistake? When he plays the role of the other party and uses the devil's advocate method, he'll ask a lot of these same questions, as well as take the opposing side of every issue you raise.

The purpose of this exercise is to prepare yourself for any doubts, concerns, and misgivings your counterpart may bring up. Having the answers ahead of time makes it easier to reassure the other party that you have thought everything through. It also makes it harder for you to be caught off guard.

Bargain Hunting

Most Americans feel uncomfortable about haggling over prices. We accept the price we're given—it's part of our culture. In fact, even when it's expected for us to do so, as with buying cars and houses, we still feel uncomfortable with the haggling process. This is probably due to our lack of practicing the art, which many countries have mastered by way of street bazaars and popular marketplaces. Instead, we tend to practice the art of *giving money away* at casinos in Las Vegas and Atlantic City!

It's a misconception to think that only big-ticket items should be negotiated. Keep in mind that every time you see a price tag, it can be changed. While you'll have a difficult time getting a price reduction in major retail stores, such as Old Navy or JC Penney, there are plenty of places for you to go and plenty of circumstances to take advantage of.

Flea Markets and Yard Sales

Without a doubt, these are two of the best resources for practicing your negotiating skills. Wherever and whenever there's a flea market or yard sale, you can expect the area's most highly proficient dealmakers to flock to the site. And expect them early! Before the sun even has a chance to rise, bargain hunters are already at the doorstep, waiting for vendors to bring out their goods. The reason for this is because the best selection is available first thing in the morning when no one has had a chance to pick through items or buy them in bulk. Another reason these buyers show up early is because they usually have a full day of flea markets, yard sales, estate sales, and other sites to visit so they try to get to each place as early as possible.

FACT

Other places to practice haggling include roadside booths for baked goods or flowers, antique shows, furniture galleries, flooring galleries, bookstores, jewelers, pawn shops, hotels, consignment shops, and specialty shops.

When you're ready to enter the world of extreme bargaining, arrive at your destination early to get the best experience. Once inside, pick one of the early birds to "shadow." Discreetly follow this expert from vendor to vendor, observing the exchanges that are made. Listen to the negotiations. Make note of how this person talks the price down as well as voice inflections, body language, and tactics. How much time does the haggler spend talking with the vendor before starting to talk about price? What about negotiating style? What is the vendor's style? Are they friendly toward each other, or are the conversations strictly business? Are the results of their negotiation fair?

After you've observed a couple of different people, go to as many tables as you can to experience a good variety of negotiating styles and a well-rounded perspective of different personality types. Before you begin, here are a few tips the experts use:

- Pay attention to how the vendor interacts with potential customers. If she's pleasant, you can probably get a fair price from her. If she has a defensive attitude and isn't friendly, you might want to try your luck with another vendor.

- Notice whether the vendor is willing to negotiate or if she turns a lot of people away. Chances are that if she almost never comes down on price, you probably won't be able to practice your skills with her. You might want to check back with her toward the end of the day when she's eager to get as many sales as possible.

- Determine how well the vendor knows her products by listening to her answers to shoppers' questions. If she seems uncomfortable giving information, she probably doesn't know that much. Usually, if a person doesn't know the details about what she's selling, she won't negotiate with you because she doesn't want to get ripped off.

- When buying more than a few items from one vendor, ask for a discount. If you're unable to talk down the prices of the items you want to buy, try getting 10–15 percent off the total sale. If a vendor senses that she's about to lose a big sale, she'll more than likely find a way to compensate you.

- Compare prices from one vendor to the next on similar items. Most flea markets feature vendors that sell the same products; for instance, there could be ten different booths selling the same computer software. Negotiate with each vendor, but don't buy right away. If one vendor says she'll sell you something for $40, use that as leverage for when you negotiate with the next vendor. Keep using this strategy until you get the best deal.

To get the most out of your experience, visit a few different flea markets and yard sales. The Web site *www.fleamarketguide.com* lists locations of flea markets by state along with hours of operation. To locate yard sales, check your local newspaper for listings.

Festivals, Parades, and Fairs

Festivals, parades, and fairs often include an assortment of booths where trinkets, clothing, art, jewelry, fragrances, candles, incense, and soaps are sold by vendors who, in keeping with the theme of the event, may be dressed in gypsy, pirate, or Renaissance costumes waiting for the next passerby to strike up a deal. Most of the vendors are open to bargaining and will give you great deals toward the end of the day when no one seems to be interested in buying.

If you really want to get a feel for how bartering was done in the past, attending one or two of these galas will no doubt get you in the spirit, not to mention provide you with a fun experience.

eBay

To get in some extra practice, visit *www.ebay.com* and start bargaining with other Internet users for anything that piques your interest. These days you can find virtually anything from antique dolls to themed lunch boxes up for sale on this site. You can guarantee that someone out there would give his left foot to have one of the items you've stored in a box labeled "junk."

Here's how eBay works. You search for an item by keyword or category. Look at the asking price, see what other people have bid on the item, and make your own bid. A date is posted telling when the auction will close, and you receive notification via e-mail if you win the bid. If you've never been on this Web site before, read the easy-to-follow instructions on the home page and start bidding away.

At the Restaurant

A restaurant is a great place to start exercising your self-confidence because you have plenty of opportunities to ask for what you want. Employees are usually eager to please. Your servers want a good tip, so they are concerned about your satisfaction with service; the kitchen staff doesn't want to gain a reputation for cooking bad food, so they want you to enjoy your meal; and the management wants more people to go to the restaurant, so they count on your enjoyment of the dining experience to make you spread the word about how great it was.

Be Seated

When you get to the restaurant, ask the host or hostess for a specific table. If it's really busy, you probably won't be accommodated, but it certainly doesn't hurt to ask, especially when you're in negotiating training. Some other specifics you can ask for include the following:

- Being seated away from the entrance door, kitchen, and restrooms
- Being seated at a booth instead of a table
- Being seated outdoors instead of indoors
- Being seated next to a window
- Being seated in a corner for privacy

Getting these concessions may seem like small successes, but the feeling you get after having your request fulfilled is a positive one. Further, if you follow the next few steps successfully, you'll begin to feel like royalty when you continuously get your way.

Ordering Your Meal

When your server comes to take your order, ask for something that's not on the menu. You can give any reason you like (you're in the mood for something else, you don't like the menu choices, or you're on a special diet), as long as you don't give up. If the server says "no" right off the bat, gather your things as if you're going to leave. At that point, she'll realize she's about to lose her tip and will probably tell you that she'll talk to the manager about it to see what she can do.

Another thing you can do is build your own meal. If an entrée comes with two sides, ask the server if you can substitute the sides with two meatless items from the appetizer list. Explain that you don't want the full-size appetizers; you want the portions to be the same size as the original sides. If you discover you'll have to pay a little extra to do that, ask if you can have a larger portion of the entrée.

ALERT!

Don't forget to negotiate concession for concession in every situation. In the previous example, you're getting the same amount of food (because you chose two meatless items), but you are being charged extra because you ordered from the appetizer menu. However, you asked that they be the same portion size as the original entrée sides, so in this case you should get something in return for the extra money you're paying.

Paying for Your Meal

Last but not least, paying for the meal is something that should always be negotiated if you had a bad experience in one area of service. If your server took your order wrong, forgot to bring you drinks, or served your food cold, these are all reasons for getting a discount off the total bill. If the meat you ordered was bad, the soda you received was flat, or if there was a hair somewhere on the plate, those items should come off the bill and you should get a major discount on the total.

If you order something on the menu and the server comes back to tell you that they're out of that item, ask for a discount on what you choose to replace it with. This shows that you're still willing to have a meal at the restaurant even though what you want isn't available. If the establishment can't compensate you for your trouble, then why should you ever come back? Once you start to leave, the server will get the manager, who is sure to do whatever it takes to make you happy. Any restaurant manager would rather have 85 percent of the price of the meal than nothing at all.

Going Shopping

Instead of thinking about bargaining as something that takes up too much time and energy, think of it as an unwritten rule that very few people know about. If you knew you could get a good deal every time you bought something, wouldn't you? How many times have you thumbed through the pile of flyers in your local Sunday newspaper, searching for the best price on the software you want to buy for your computer? Do you shop only when stores are having sales?

It seems almost impossible to stretch your dollars when everything you want to buy has a set price. Why do we continue to settle for prices that we don't think are fair? After all, we're the consumers—shouldn't we be able to have some control over the standard? You have more control than you think. All you need is a good reason and a little creative thinking to get the price you want to pay.

If you can't get a reduction on an item you think is priced too high, and you're purchasing other items, try to get a discount off the total sale. Show how much you plan on spending at the store and how they will lose out on the entire sale if you can't get a fair price.

The Big Secret

Getting to that price involves knowing a little something about how retail works. When buyers purchase items for a store or other venue, they get them at a discounted price because they are buying in bulk. Also, other arrangements might have been made, such as agreements to make a certain amount of purchases in the future. The buyer then works with company or venue seniors (and sometimes the marketing department) to determine what the retail prices will be. Though the markups on items vary from product to product and store to store, the price you see on the tag is probably 50 to 70 percent higher than the original price. If the buyer purchased a sweater for $15, the price will be between $22.50 and $25.50.

Armed with this information, you should no longer feel hesitant, unjustified, or embarrassed about asking for (and getting!) a discount on whatever your heart desires.

Some retailers simply will not budge on price. That's usually because they don't have the authority to adjust prices. However, managers do make exceptions and mark down items that are damaged or part of a set in which the other piece is missing.

Any time you have film developed, no matter where it is, ask about their policy regarding photos that don't come out the way you wanted them to. Most of us aren't professional photographers. We sometimes end up with one or two photos with a fingertip in the way, a blur of colors, or an underexposed image because we forgot to use the flash. You shouldn't have to pay for these, and if you do, you can find another place to have your film developed.

Another way to get a discount is to buy the shelf model of an item instead of getting it in the box. Inspect it carefully before making the decision to buy it, and then come up with a number to give the sales associate. Never pay full price for a shelf model—it's been handled, moved, and played with since the day it was put out, so it's probably not in pristine condition. Nevertheless, it is still functional, and a lot of people are able to afford electronics and save a few hard-earned dollars by purchasing shelf models.

ALERT!

Don't get greedy. The goal of bargaining or haggling with retailers isn't to see if you can get away with something. Remember, you want to be proactive in price control, and as a consumer, it's your basic right. Train yourself not to take prices at face value, but don't nickel-and-dime every chance you get. Research the market, and set a price you think is reasonable for both you and the retailer.

Price Matching

One marketing strategy that's been popping up everywhere involves advertising a price for an item and challenging customers to find a better one elsewhere. If you can find a lower price, the retailer invites you to go to their store, where they'll gladly lower their price to match the one you found at the competition. Home Depot and Lowe's engage in this type of marketing to attract customers into their stores "just to see" what their prices are like. For example, if you want to get the best price on a front door, you'll have to go into Home Depot to get a quote. Once there, the retailer hopes you'll look around to check out their current sales and new products. Next, you'll go to Lowe's to get a comparison price, and while you're there you might see something you need on sale.

Price matching actually works out in your favor because it encourages you to research the market for the best price on whatever it is you want to buy. Even if the store where you're buying doesn't openly participate in the strategy, you can use it to negotiate a better price anyway. Tell them you saw the door at a lower price somewhere else, and if they can't match it you'll go there to buy it. Take advantage of the game, and you'll never have to wonder whether you could've gotten a better deal somewhere else.

Using Competitor's Coupons

Coupons are little jewels that can save you a lot of money—if you can remember to use them. If you see a coupon for something you regularly buy, cut it out, even if it's not the brand you like. Some grocery stores accept competitor's coupons and give you the discount even if the item you're buying is not exactly the same. Some also accept coupons that are specifically for one store because it means getting you to go into their store instead. The fifty-cent discount on toilet paper is a small concession to make for a $50 grocery purchase that they otherwise might not have had.

Remember, every retailer wants your business, so they will usually do whatever it takes to get it. This gives you the upper hand because your options are endless; you can easily go to the competitor up the street to get the price you want. Use coupons to negotiate a discount every chance you get, and keep track of how much money you save each month.

At Work

You can try out your new skills at the office in a variety of ways. Each of the following activities will you give the opportunity to practice the various stages of negotiating:

Planning stage (goals and objectives)—Volunteer to be the designated party planner for birthdays, baby showers, and happy hours. Goals can include deciding on what type of party to have (breakfast get-together, luncheon, after-work appetizers), what kind of food to bring, and how to decorate for the theme.

Research stage (background information)—For birthday parties, you'll want to do some investigating about the person whose birthday it is so you can create a theme around her interests and avoid including something she dislikes. For happy hours, find a few different places near the office and visit them to see what kinds of diversions (pool tables, dart boards, big-screen televisions), food specials (two-for-one appetizers, party platters), and drink specials they have.

Finding common ground—Get a feel for what kind of food and snacks the majority likes, as well as input on where people would like to have the next celebration. If you work in an office where most people don't drink alcohol, you'll need to find a place for happy hour that's appropriate for their needs.

Having alternatives—Create a list of ideas and pass it around the office so people can add to it. This gets everyone involved and keeps things interesting.

Creating agendas—Everyone's schedule is different, so coordinating them will be challenging. There will always be a few people who can't show up, so pick a date that fits into the majority's schedules.

Chapter 17

A Lifetime of Negotiating Strategies

Many of life's milestones include opportunities for negotiation, but things get complicated when emotions run high—after all, the results will have a major impact on the rest of your life. This chapter takes you through some of life's biggest challenges using the steps we've outlined in this book: knowing who's involved, preparing for the big day, and strategies for a win/win solution.

Negotiating a Salary

Do your homework before presenting your case. The information can be your leverage and will give you the courage and strength to tackle the issue with confidence. Like any good negotiation, the time you put into it *before-hand* determines the success of the outcome. Here's what you'll need to consider before making your move:

- **The opportunity**—How does the job fit into your career goals? Will you be making a lateral move, or will you be taking the next step upward on your career path?
- **Job duties**—Do you have the skills required for the position? Will it be challenging enough? What responsibilities will you have? Is there room for advancement? Are you going to like doing the job?
- **The company**—What kind of history does it have? Do you agree with its philosophies and values? Is it successful, and is it growing toward an even more successful future?

There's no doubt that negotiating your salary is a scary process, especially when the job bank is close to being spent. It's also easy to underestimate your worth and jump at the first offer just to get the job, but you'd be doing yourself more harm than good if you chose this route.

- **Salary**—What is the going rate for the position? What is your worth in the marketplace? How does what you're being offered compare to your previous job? What is your ideal number? Based on your budget, what number must you absolutely have? What are you willing to settle for?
- **Benefits and perks**—Are the health, dental, and life insurance plans attractive? Is a 401(k) plan being offered? How much paid time off will you receive? What other benefits and perks are available (child care, expense account, tuition reimbursement, bonuses, company car)?

- **Lifestyle**—How does the position affect the quality of your life? Will you be away from home a lot (frequently working overtime, required to travel)? Is the long drive worth it? Will you have to relocate?

These elements are worth more together, as a total package, than they are separately. However, the information you gather about each issue gives you more to negotiate with and allows you to be more flexible. Probably the most significant data is a pay-comparison report. A generic report is free, but to get a more personal report, tailored to your own work history, it'll usually run you about $40 or $50. The following Web sites provide both free and extensive reports:

- *www.salary.com*
- *www.salaryexpert.com*
- *www.monster.com*
- *www.careerjournal.com*
- *www.jobsmart.org*
- *http://salary.hotjobs.com*

FACT

It's a good idea to look at as many comparisons as you can, since you may not be able to find the specific job title you're looking for right away. Most sites provide you with the job duties involved in each position, so if you can't find the title you're looking for, match the job description instead.

Now that you've done the research, it's time to gather all the positive energy you have and give it your best shot. Regardless of how much or how little experience you have, what matters most now is your knowledge of the market—both in your field and in the employment industry as a whole.

Start Negotiating

Find out if the person you'll be interviewing with is a supervisor, director, or vice president. This will determine what types of decisions the interviewer is allowed to make. Next, highlight all the skills that advanced you further in your previous jobs, including those that reflect your ability to learn fast. Estimate timeframes for your achievements to show how quickly you can adapt to the position.

When it's finally time to discuss salary, get a number before you give one (even just a range or an estimate). Never be the first to make an offer. The reason for this is twofold. If your offer is too high, you could be overlooked because other candidates produced a lower number for the employer to negotiate with. If your offer is too low, you'll get taken advantage of.

Then counter the offer by giving your range, *not* a single number. Use the high number of their range as the low number of your range and try to get a little above that number if possible. As mentioned previously, use benefits and perks as compensation for not getting the exact number you want. Can you negotiate an extra day off per month, a few extra personal days, and a sign-on bonus?

ALERT!

The biggest mistake people make when negotiating salary is that they don't have the slightest idea of what they're worth, what they have the right to ask for, or the value of benefits and perks.

Remember, salary isn't the most important aspect of acquiring a new position. Look at the whole picture, and adjust each element as needed to get the best deal possible. Then compare the package with what other companies are offering to determine how well you'll fare.

Asking for a Raise

It's always difficult to ask for a raise—for one thing, we're often afraid we'll be fired for being so bold. You might feel that if you really do a great job, your boss should come to you with a pay increase, not the other way around. But it's simply not in your boss's best interest to give you a raise unless you ask for it. Luckily, there's a way to approach the subject without having to fear immediate termination. It begins with the realization that your boss isn't always aware of the great job you're doing.

Before you approach your boss, do some salary-comparison research, and reassess your benefits package. Then make a list of all your achievements and produce hard evidence that shows how your work has made an impact on the company. Gather any documentation of positive feedback you've received from superiors and peers in other departments as well as your own. Also, be prepared to counter any flaws, such as days you were late or left early, mistakes that were made, and so on. Don't get defensive or upset. Your boss knows that nobody's perfect, and she might just be looking for an explanation.

When you're ready to meet with your boss, choose an appropriate time to discuss the issue, such as during your performance review or at a scheduled time and place. Don't knock on your boss's door and expect a meeting right then and there. Also, don't approach him during the company's busy season when he is likely to be working hard and probably crunched for time.

In the Market for a Car

Once again, the more time you take to educate yourself about what you're trying to achieve, the more favorable an outcome you'll have. In the business of automobiles, you'll be working with master negotiators—salesmen, sales managers, finance and insurance managers—who have honed their skills to perfection. As frightful as that may sound, you can still get your way by being informed and staying focused.

Making an informed decision about price involves being aware of all the things that affect the bottom line. If you're undecided about whether you want to buy a new car, buy a used car, or lease a car, figuring out the numbers for each option will help you choose which one is right for you.

Buying a New Car

When buying a new car, there are a few terms you'll want to know about before you begin negotiating with a salesman:

- **List price**—Manufacturer's suggested retail price (MSRP)
- **Invoice price**—Actual price of the car as seen on the factory invoice that's billed to the dealer
- **Hold-back**—Portion of the invoice price that the factory holds back and refunds to dealer when cars are sold
- **Factory-to-dealer cash payments**—Payments made to dealers when certain cars are sold at certain times
- **Customer rebates**—Money that the manufacturer gives the customer. This money is yours, no matter what, so don't let it be included in the negotiation.
- **Front-end profits**—The amount of profit made from the sale, which in turn pays sales commission
- **Back-end profits**—Add-ons usually sold by the financing manager, including extended warranties, rust protection, fabric protection, special painting, and so on
- **Wholesale value**—Value of a car (your trade-in) to someone (dealership) who will resell it for a profit

Once you have all these facts, you'll be able to determine the true price of a car. Next, figure out how much you're willing to put down, what kind of finance rate you can expect to get, and which finance option is best for you.

FACT

To get an accurate appraisal on your trade-in, pick up a copy of the *Kelley Blue Book* as well as a copy of the *National Auto Research Black Book*. The numbers might be different in each book, but at least you can get a range and decide where to go from there.

Your strategy is to reveal nothing. Don't tell the salesperson how you plan to pay, what finance option you want, whether you're using your current car as a trade-in, or how much you love the car. Stay in control, and talk only about the car you're interested in and its true cost. Every issue should be dealt with separately after the price of the car is determined. Counter every tactic by remembering that you must stay in control and be firm and confident about what you want. If the salesman tries to get you to commit early ("If I throw in a few extra options, will you take this price?"), simply tell him that you're not sure and you'd like to look at the final numbers before making a decision. If he tells you that other people are interested in the car, but he'll hold it for you if you make a deposit on it, don't fall for it. As soon as you hand over that money, you lose control. Besides, if you find a better deal somewhere else, your deposit money will be tied up.

Salespeople love to use the flattery tactic to soften you up. They tell you how much they enjoy working with someone who knows what they want and has done their research, and then they get you to trust them by swearing to be completely honest with you. Avoid flaunting what you know; it only gives the salesperson the opportunity to take control. Car dealerships also use the good guy/bad guy tactic, in which the salesperson is the one on your side and the boss is the one who keeps rejecting all your offers. Threaten to leave if this goes on too long or else you'll end up wasting your whole day at one dealership.

QUESTION?

What is Fighting Chance?

It's a customer information service that gives you access to hold-back data, dealer and consumer incentives, invoice figures, sales figures, and other records. It costs $19.95 plus $3 for shipping and is well worth the money because all the information is current. Visit ✍*www.fighting chance.com* or call ✆(800) 288-1134 for more information.

Buying a Used Car

If you have your eye on a used car, make sure you know the wholesale price before anything else. Dealers mark up the prices significantly on used cars so it appears as if you got a good deal when they give you a few thousand dollars off the price. You'll also want to have the car inspected—inside and out—for any major problems that could end up costing you in the future. Stay calm when negotiating, and never settle for anything above your maximum price. One strategy you might want to use is to have the money right then and there. The dealer is sure to give you a fair price if he knows he can have a guaranteed sale.

Leasing a Car

Leasing can save you a lot of money in the long run if you shop around for the best deal. If you're considering a lease instead of a purchase, comparing the *money factor* (the fee the company charges you for "renting" the car) to the interest rate of the loan on a purchase can help you make up your mind. Use price guides to figure out the *cap cost* (equal to the selling price) and evaluate the *cap cost reduction* (discounts dealers give off the list price).

You'll also want to find out about the term of the lease (shouldn't exceed the length of manufacturer's warranty), cost of additional miles, early termination fees, gap insurance (covers you if car is stolen before the end of the lease), purchase options, deficiency (difference between what you owe on the car and the cash value of the car—the amount you'll have to pay if you terminate the lease early), and minimum requirements for insurance coverage.

Once you have all this information, you're ready to deal. However, as mentioned earlier, don't let the salesman know your intent. Negotiate the price of the car before you tell him you want to lease.

Getting a Divorce

This is one of the most difficult negotiations to endure. At an extremely emotional point, you have to learn how to let it all go and put on a professional face. How do you negotiate when all you want to do is burst out into tears or yell at the person sitting across from you? First, consider using a mediator (instead of a lawyer) to help you through the negotiation process. Once you've chosen the person you'll be working with, set clear goals so you stay on track and get through it with the fewest scars possible.

With the Help of a Mediator

Most couples prefer to use mediators because of their successful track record. Where lawyers tend to be cold, self-serving, one-sided, and inaccessible, mediators are compassionate. They work to serve the clients, hold an impartial opinion, and are there when you need them.

FACT

Couples are more likely to carry out the terms of an agreement settled during mediation than in court because they have more control over the conditions and can allow for more flexibility. Judges are required to follow rigid state laws when handling divorces, whereas mediation allows you to decide on all the details.

One of the biggest factors for choosing a mediator is that it saves couples thousands of dollars in court costs. Further, mediators listen to both sides of an argument and work with both parties to determine the best possible outcome. They help couples devise alternate solutions to messy problems, solutions they wouldn't have been able to see on their own because of their emotional states.

If you choose to use a mediator, know that you'll still need to hire a lawyer to draw up the separation agreement. Usually, the mediator creates a draft of the agreement that lists all the points discussed, and the lawyer uses that as a guide to devise the formal document. After everyone signs the paperwork, a divorce hearing is held (which you may or may not have to attend) and the judge declares the divorce final.

What Needs to Be Worked Out

First, you and your spouse need to decide on a meeting place. If you're using a mediator, this will usually be her office. Next, create an agenda. Limit the time to no more than a few hours—any more and you risk exhaustion, which has the tendency to cause emotional outbreaks.

> During the process, you'll have several meetings, each with its own agenda. This type of schedule is meant to keep everyone focused on the goals you need to accomplish in order to come to an agreement and make the divorce final. This is especially difficult when children are involved because arrangements have to be made for their care.

Although each divorce is unique, the issues you need to discuss may include the following:

- Division of property and assets
- Custody schedule
- Child support
- Alimony
- Taxes
- Parental responsibilities, including who stays home when a child is sick
- Plans for the future, such as setting money aside for a child's college fund

The solution to a successful negotiation is to remain calm and civil. If your spouse starts delivering personal attacks or gets angry, don't be antagonized. As difficult as it will be, your best move is to remain silent. Once it is plain that you're not reacting, the negotiation will eventually get back to the issues. Additionally, encourage agreement by acknowledging when your spouse has given something to you, such as every Thanksgiving with the kids.

Time to Get a Cell Phone

Choosing a cell phone plan isn't as major as buying a home or automobile, but it is a long process that involves just as much planning, skill, and determination. Because cell phone companies usually lock you into long contracts, it only makes sense to shop around for the best of what the market has to offer. The following is a list of all the features you'll want to find out about:

- Type of phone that's being offered and its features
- Length of contract
- Minutes in your plan (nights, weekends, peak, off-peak, rollover)
- Long-distance and over-minutes rate
- Coverage areas and analog frequencies
- Service activation fees
- National vs. regional plans, flexible plans, rollover plans, mobile-to-mobile plans
- How long you'll have to cancel if you're not happy (most states give two weeks)

Round One

First, call each company and get a list of everything they have to offer. Create a spreadsheet to record all perks and benefits and how long each offer will be available. Highlight the best deals under each category, and prepare for your next round of calls.

Round Two

Get a list of Round Two offers using the best offers you got from your Round One calls as leverage. For example, you might say, "Your competitor offered me a better phone and a lower long-distance rate. If you're not willing to give me that, can you give me X-amount of minutes and a shorter contract?" Keep going until you feel you have the best of what everyone is offering.

ALERT!

Remember not to give something up unless you get something in return. If the person you're negotiating with doesn't have the authority to give you concessions, ask to speak with someone who does, or call back and talk to a different representative.

Round Three

Your final round of calls includes contacting your current provider (if you have one) and asking them to beat the best deal you were able to obtain from the competition. Ask them what they'd be willing to do to keep you as a customer. If they can't do anything more for you, your final call will be to the company that gave you the best deal.

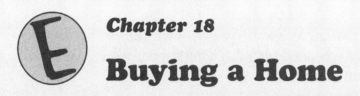

Chapter 18

Buying a Home

There are lots of negotiations involved in buying a home. You need to secure a good mortgage and agree with your family members on the location and type of housing you're looking for. Once you find the home you want to buy, the real negotiations will begin. You don't simply pay what the seller is asking. Using your negotiating skills, you'll be able to work out a better price for you that is also acceptable to the seller.

What Is Fair Market Value?

You will have to determine fair price of the home you want before you make an offer for it. This is defined as the highest price a ready, willing, and able buyer will pay and the lowest a ready, willing, and able seller will accept. To be completely accurate, fair market value cannot be established until a property is actually sold. But the trick of an estimate is to come as close as possible to the figure for which you could turn around after the closing and quickly sell the house again (within three months or so—that is about how long "quickly" is in real estate).

You can make your market evaluation by comparing the property you want to buy with similar properties that have been sold in the area during the past year. You will already have a feel for the price from all the house hunting you have been doing.

When you are ready to start negotiating, ask your realty agent to show you *comparables.* The term "comparables," in a real-estate setting, refers to the listing sheets that agents have describing properties that have recently been sold. Those sheets will contain all the pertinent information on the property, including the original asking price, all price reductions, the actual selling price, the date of the closing, and the date of the original listing contract. You can use the date of the original listing to determine how long the house was on the market before it sold.

Almost every real-estate office that belongs to a multiple-listing organization will have a comparables file or a computerized comparables book. Even independent agencies that do not share listings will keep a file of properties sold by their own offices and agents. The single-office file works well in large cities where many brokers are independents and tend to work only in tightly defined neighborhoods rather than trying to cover the entire city. It also works well in condo or co-op sales, where one or two real-estate agencies usually handle all the sales within a particular building.

After you have seen comparables, make a list of selling prices and addresses of the properties that you consider similar to "yours." Take home photocopies of those listing sheets, if the agent is willing and allowed to give them to you. Compare and rate each property against the house you want to make an offer on.

When you finish that homework, you will know exactly what other people in the area have had to pay for a certain amount of house in the same or a similar neighborhood. From here, stepping along to an evaluation of what "your" house is worth is relatively easy.

Once you have determined what you think is a fair selling price for the property, compare it with what the sellers are asking. If your evaluation price is higher than the asking price (that rarely occurs), do not get out your pen to sign an offer. Look again at the property, the neighborhood, the location, the lot, the time on the market, local conditions—everything. You may have missed something very important. However, if everything checks out, then act quickly. The sellers may just have under priced their property; so, buy before word gets out and another buyer appears and starts a bidding war.

It is much more likely that the asking price will be more than your estimate of fair market value. That is what negotiating is all about. Put yourself in the sellers' shoes for a moment. Why do you think they set the price so high? To allow room for negotiating? Because they have installed new carpeting? They want to be repaid for their newly remodeled $14,000 kitchen? Take the position that the amenities or upgrades do not always add to the resale value of a home.

You would be smart to buy a small notebook for this process, and make it your negotiating journal. Record the addresses and prices of your comparables. Then record your ideal price for the home you want, your estimate of its fair market value, and the top price you're willing to pay. Keep the journal on hand as you go through the negotiating process to help determine how much you want to raise your offer.

You should figure out your ideal price for the home (likely to be a "steal" price), your estimate of fair market value, and your absolute "top-dollar" price. Gee, you ask, why would I want to pay a top-dollar price that is higher than the fair market value of the property? Because until the contract is signed, the fair market value is still an estimate, and even professional real-estate appraisers can differ in their fair market value estimates. Therefore, you must leave yourself a margin of error, a realistic dollar space that will keep you from becoming too rigid during the negotiations.

Most important of all during this negotiating stage is that you do not tell your real-estate agent your "top-dollar figure"—or your "steal" figure either. Remember, the agent represents the seller. If you tell the agent that you are willing to go up to as high as $123,000 for a house listed at $125,000, then $123,000 is probably what you will end up paying. You have to play your hand close to the vest during the negotiating process, even with your agent.

QUESTION?

What if I'm no good at negotiating?
Relax, it's not as scary as it may sound. If you are using a real-estate agent, he or she will be your go-between. You won't be talking directly to the seller in most cases.

The Market at the Moment

Besides checking comparables and working the numbers, it is important that you gauge the state of the market in your area at the time you want to buy. For example, if it is a hot sellers' market, where properties are moving quickly, and the home you want is a desirable one with potentially wide market appeal, start your negotiations fairly close to market value. You do not want to lose the property playing games over price.

In some situations, although this is uncommon, a house or a location is so "hot" that simultaneous offers are made. Sometimes the best of these is simply accepted, with no negotiating. More often the sellers negotiate with all prospective buyers simultaneously. They are "out for the kill." If you truly want that property in such a situation, here are some tactics that will help:

- Offer your best price, but be willing to move up another $500 or $1,000. Do not, however, get caught up in auction-fever and bid the house up far above its market value.
- Ask for as few extras in the sale as possible.
- Make the closing date as agreeable to the sellers as you can.
- Have loan approval from a mortgage lender.

On the other hand, if the market is soft where you are looking (sometimes called a buyers' market), if the seller is under need-to-sell stress, or if the house is not particularly appealing to most people—they cannot see the potential that you can, or their needs are different from yours—you can move more slowly and negotiate over a wider range. In these situations, it is possible to get a much better deal with a bit of patience and perseverance.

Your Initial Offer

You may hear people say that 10 percent below asking price is a good first offer. It isn't, really. There is no one "good" initial offer based upon asking price. Why? Because there are so many variables in real estate and because sellers rarely set their asking prices with consideration to market value or other rational thought processes. They want to get the most they can for their properties, and many have emotional ties to their homes that turn simple Cape Cods into mental castles. Would you offer 10 percent less than the asking price of a home that is overpriced by $25,000 or more?

Each and every piece of real property is unique, and so is each selling situation. So, you can understand why generic rules of thumb in real estate are dangerous. But if you must have a guideline, a first offer that is 10 percent below your fair market value estimate—not the seller's asking price—will keep you from insulting the seller. It will also keep you from having your first offer snapped up because it was higher than the seller thought he would actually get for the property.

So now you have a figure in mind for your first offer. How do you go about making that offer?

What is earnest money?
Earnest money is a sum of money that you provide along with your offer that demonstrates to the seller the seriousness of your intent to buy.

Your offer cannot just be verbal. Most residential sales agents will refuse to present a verbal offer to the seller that is not accompanied by an earnest money check and specific information on financing, closing date, and other details of the sale. A buyer cannot call an agent and say, "Ask them if they'll take $139,500." That buyer could be asking the same question of four different agents about four different properties, a situation that can end up presenting serious problems. Your offer must be presented to the sellers in writing.

When your real-estate agent hears the word *offer*, he or she might whip out a binder, a short form that includes your name and address, a few lines about the property being bid on, and the amount of your earnest money deposit (usually $500 or $1,000). If you are handed a binder, be certain it contains the clause "subject to review by the buyer's attorney within five business days." That will allow you to have your lawyer look over the form (and will also allow you an out if you change your mind about that property).

The Counteroffer

The counteroffer is the seller's response to your initial bid. Sometimes it names the actual amount they want for the property, but not usually. Most sellers still have some room in their first-response prices, even when they say, "Not a penny less." You now must work toward a meeting of the minds.

In your negotiating journal, record your first offer, its terms, and its contingencies (or have your agent give you a copy of the offer form after it is completely filled out and signed). When you get the counteroffer, record not only its facts and figures but also what the agent says the sellers said. Do they want a quick closing? Is this their bottom price? Are they anxious to sell? Do not take a word of what you hear as gospel truth, though. In negotiating, you must always keep testing for what is "real" and what is just a negotiation tactic. The counteroffer is usually returned to you on your original offer form, with numbers crossed out and new numbers written in and initialed.

Most agents will want you to sign a contract before they present your offer to the seller. If you sign the contract, and if the sellers agree to your offer and also sign that form, you have bought the house.

Your Second Offer

Your second offer should not be your top dollar, but it should be closer to your estimate of the market value. Have the agent write out a whole new offer form. Do not work with scratched-out figures and initials on the original sheet, since this will only confuse people.

Add to your negotiating journal the facts of this second offer and any asides that are mentioned by anyone. Keeping such a written account of who said what and when may prevent arguments, misunderstandings, and denials later. It will also give you a chance to review what happened throughout the process.

At each step of the bidding, it is worth mentioning to your real-estate agent the flaws of the house—something to the effect that of course you like and want the house, but it does need kitchen remodeling, or you really wanted a two-car, not a one-car, garage. You want your agent to know—and relay to the sellers—that you are not so committed to this house that you will pay anything to own it. There are other homes out there that could suit you, too. Even though you may feel this is the perfect house for you, if the sellers knows that, they will have the upper hand in the negotiating, and you are likely to pay a higher price for it.

As You Move Toward Agreement

Most homes are sold upon or before the buyers' third offer. Sometimes, however, the negotiating goes on for many days. The procedure is always the same—offer, counteroffer. You and the sellers are making adjustments, circling about each other, and trying to find a place to meet. Here is where the advice of a good realty agent can be invaluable!

Keep Your Emotions in Check

Getting emotional—whether the emotion is on either the buyer's or seller's side—can heat up the negotiating process to the point where the real-estate agent wants to run for cover! This is not good. Acting rationally is essential when you are negotiating to buy a home. Here are the most common emotions that carry away both buyers and sellers.

Love

For you, this means love of the house you are negotiating for, but you should try not to fall head over heels for it. If you start thinking that this is the only house for you and that you will never find another house as good anywhere, you might as well forget about negotiating effectively. Try to remember there are other houses that will suit you just as well—and maybe better—even if you haven't found them yet.

If you lose the house you love, and you have the luxury of time, it is a good idea to wait a while before going out house-hunting again. You do not want to buy on the rebound if you can avoid it. Purchasing the wrong house is a costly mistake.

Anger

This emotion makes an appearance in most real-estate negotiations at some point or another. The buyers may get angry at the sellers, the sellers may get angry at the buyers, they both can get angry at the real-estate agent(s), and the agent(s) can get angry at them. Buying a house can be stressful, and no one wants to be taken advantage of.

It might be hard to stay calm and rational, but that should be your mantra during the negotiating process. Here are some suggestions for doing just that:

- **Use time for cooling off.** If you feel yourself (or your spouse) about to scream, say, "I'd (we'd) like to take some time to think about this before saying anything more." Hang up the phone, leave the room, or leave town for the day if you have to.
- **Define the cause of your anger.** People sometimes find themselves furious without knowing why. Ask yourselves, "What got this started?" Once you answer that question, it is easier to say, "How can we settle this?"
- **Stick to the point.** If you are negotiating over a closing date, do not let who is going to fix the broken toilet get into the discussion.
- **Do not slam doors or burn bridges.** It is hard to come back from "Take your stupid house and stuff it."
- **Do not accuse.** "This is all your fault" gets you nowhere. Ask instead, "How did we get to this point, and where should we go from here?"
- **Do not lie.** Never lie—not at all, over anything. If you said something yesterday and changed your mind overnight, say so. Do not deny what you said. Do not fib about your financial situation—you will be found out anyway. Conveniently "forgetting" something counts as a lie here, too. Nothing sours a deal faster than contradictions about money.
- **Do not pound your fist on the table, and do not raise your voice.** Your point can be made without throwing a fit. Speak so softly that your listeners will have to listen harder.

Pride

Many a real-estate deal has been lost over a comment like, "No way! They're not going to have the last word! No way!" So, no sale. Negotiating is not a game of winning or losing. It is a coming together. You have to be able to give up a little to get a little.

Possessiveness and Greed

Sometimes it is difficult for sellers to part emotionally with their property. Some fight to keep every stick that is not nailed down, and they expect to be paid dearly for every one that is. That could be seen as possessiveness.

When people buy, however, they want the most for their money. "That should go with the house" is the usual attitude, since they are anticipating the out-of-pocket expenses for everything that does not go with the house. That could be seen as greed. There is no right answer here. If you get into an argument over bits and pieces, ask yourself if possessiveness or greed are not factors. Sometimes just recognizing those feelings helps to resolve the issue.

Negotiating with FSBOs

When you're dealing with homes that are "for sale by owner" (or FSBOs), no real-estate agent is involved in the negotiations. The same principles for negotiating apply, but there is, of course, no middle man.

How do you begin the negotiations? After your second visit to the home you like (the visit where you have explored the house more thoroughly than you did on your initial visit), wait a day or two before making an offer, to heighten the sellers' anticipation and to make your offer sound well thought out.

ALERT!

Get a lawyer to help with a "for sale by owner" deal. You should always have a lawyer in a case where there is no real-estate agent involved, but do *not* use the same legal counsel as the sellers use.

To determine fair market value, go through computer printout sheets you have secured from real-estate agents for similar properties in the neighborhood. The bargaining process is similar in this case to bargaining through a real-estate agent, but sitting down face-to-face with sellers is always difficult. Keep rational and friendly, and remember that your primary tool for acceptance is that fair market value. Your offer hands them a quick sale, no more disruption in having a house on the market, and no sales commission to pay.

Still, they probably will not accept your first price. So, back you come with a second bid. That should usually be the fair market value minus the usual real-estate commission in the area (probably 6 or 7 percent). Of course, the sellers aren't using an agent, so there is no commission to be paid here.

In the best possible scenario, the buyer and seller will split the amount of the real-estate commission and set the selling price between market value and the price the owner would have netted after paying an agent's commission (if they had used one). All of the extras, such as closing dates and financing, can be worked out then and there, or with the attorneys for both sides present. The attorneys will draw up the contract to buy.

That's how a neat, tidy sale works. But life does not always follow such a script. The sellers may be new to this business and hold out high hopes for a top-dollar price. When you come up against a stone wall, do not beat your head against it, no matter how much you like the house. Write down your best offer, with your name, address, and phone number, and leave it with the sellers. Tell them to call you if they change their mind, and then continue house-hunting. You might want to keep in touch with them from time to time to ask how they are doing.

Do not make another offer, but if they do come down a little, perhaps you will be willing to go up a little. This is how negotiating works.

Also, you should never give sellers an earnest money deposit. That check should be handed to your lawyer.

Secrets of Successful Negotiating

Here is how to cleverly navigate the back and forth over price between you and the seller:

Know a property's value. There is nothing more important to successfully buying and selling real estate than knowing the market. As you negotiate, showing and telling them what comparable houses have sold for will help you to bring the sellers' price down. Of course, the real-estate agent will probably be doing this for you, but do not ever count on anyone else to fight for your money as diligently as you will.

Be flexible. Do not lose a property that you really want over a few dollars a month, which is what financing an extra $500 in sale price would cost you. Set limits, but do not be so rigid that you cannot respond or rethink a decision. "Never," "absolutely not," and "take it or leave it" are phrases that will slam the door on any deal.

Never show your hand. Do not tell anyone, especially not your agent (who is, remember, ultimately working for the seller, no matter how helpful he or she is to you), what you will do next. Act as if the offer you are making will be accepted. If you don't, it won't be.

Ask for concessions as you increase your bid. When you present your first offer, do not ask for extras. If it is accepted, you should have plenty of money to buy them, since your first offer was lower than total amount you have to spend. But each time you increase your offering price, ask for something more. That can be almost anything you see: chandeliers, draperies, carpeting, appliances, lawn mowers and garden equipment, lawn furniture, and sometimes even living-room or dining-room furniture. Ask as you offer. The sellers may say no to your bid but yes to your request for extras at their higher price. But when you increase your price again, even if just a little, those extras are already part of the deal in both your minds.

Never ask for all the extras at once, however. It is too overwhelming, especially with a low first offer that you are gradually increasing, as you should, in $500 or $1,000 increments. Once a seller says no, which is easy to do when the requests seem too numerous for too little money, it is harder to get a reversal than it is to get something new added later. Remember, negotiating is a give-and-take process.

Use the closing date in your negotiations. Time is money, so the saying goes. In negotiating for a home, time can be worth money if you use it as a tool. Try to find out early in the game what the sellers want out of the sale in terms of time as well as in terms of price. Do they need a quick closing because they are carrying two mortgages? Do they need time to find another house? Do they need flexibility in a closing date because they are having a house built and do not know exactly when it will be completed?

The *closing* is the date when the title of the property is actually transferred from the seller to the buyer. This date can be a valuable tool in negotiating to buy a house.

Negotiating the Closing Date

With your original low offer, you will be asked to name a closing date. If it works for you, name one that is not likely to be to the sellers' liking. If they need a quick closing, set your offer date for three or four months in the future. If they want a distant closing, ask for one in four to six weeks. Then, as you make responses to their counteroffers, you can increase the bid by very little cash but sweeten the deal by moving the proposed closing date into line with the sellers' needs. It is almost always worth money.

Other Negotiating Tactics

Use financing in your negotiations. If you plan to pay cash for your home, or if you have been preapproved by a mortgage lender, use your strong financial position as a negotiating tool. If you bid a little low, tell the agent to explain to the sellers that this is a no-risk offer. There is no mortgage contingency—the sellers don't have to wait to see if the buyers will qualify for a loan. This is a strong card!

It is typical to think that you could have negotiated better. But learn from your experience. You have done well by buying the property. You will have the opportunity to profit from your purchase. Sometimes winning is not negotiating the lowest price, but making the seller feel he or she received the best price while at the same time knowing you got a good deal, too.

Chapter 19

Negotiating with Your Kids

Your children are your pride and joy, the apple of your eye, and the toughest negotiators you'll ever have to face! They're constantly trying your patience, pleading for your consent, and arguing to get their way. These day-to-day battles can be stressful, but most things can be worked out. And just like negotiations you make in the professional world, it's essential that you keep your cool at home. This chapter is your quick reference guide for learning how to implement the steps of negotiation in your family's struggles.

Parenting Styles

Research shows there are three basic parenting styles: authoritarian, permissive, and democratic. These styles serve as guides for describing how parents deal with their children. While no parent fits into one style alone, it's important to look at these styles individually to understand how each one may be effective.

Your parenting skills are in part influenced by your own parents, other family members, and friends. And there's so much information available on good parenting, including books, magazines, and a gazillion Web sites. But ultimately, the driving force behind your parenting style lies in your own personal belief system—your values, thoughts, ethics, feelings, and opinions.

Authoritarian Ruler

This style is all about rule enforcement. Authoritarian parents want to be obeyed without question. They possess all of the control and rarely let children have a say in matters. They tell their children what to do, and the children listen. If they don't listen, the consequences are yelling, threatening, and eventually punishment. Because this type of parent is so strict, children never learn how to think for themselves. They exist inside a world with little freedom to explore, make mistakes, or learn from those mistakes.

Authoritarian parents demand respect, which in turn causes children to fear their parents. As children get older, they're more likely to rebel as they begin enjoying the feeling of freedom they never really had.

Permissive Coddler

In contrast to the authoritarian style, permissive parenting involves letting your children do whatever they want. Any rules that are made are broken time and time again because children know it can be done without any consequence. When children misbehave, the permissive parent will have a talk with them but won't enforce any punishment. Thus, children learn that they can get away with pretty much anything. Permissive parents risk raising spoiled children who are used to getting their way.

Democratic Leader

Children raised in the democratic style are taught how to be responsible because they're given choices on how to solve issues. Their opinions and feelings matter and are taken into consideration when decisions are made. Parents set reasonable rules and discuss the need for these rules with their children as well as help them understand what the consequences are for breaking them. They also provide children with plenty of options for handling problems and always incorporate their ideas into the solution.

Because these children are given the freedom to think creatively, they grow up to be independent and confident in their ability to make sound decisions. Presenting them with choices in situations where they feel helpless builds their self-esteem and lets them feel like they contribute to the family.

By using the steps of negotiation, you'll teach your children how to control their anger, calm down before the argument gets out of control, come up with solutions to the problems they are facing, and know when it's time to call in the mediators—mom and dad.

Sibling Rivalry

Brothers and sisters were born to drive each other crazy! It seems like every time you turn around they're arguing over who gets to have the one toy out of hundreds that they both want to play with at that moment. You've tried everything—yelling, punishing, taking the toy away—but they end up in the same argument the very next day. One way to break this cycle is to learn how you can teach your negotiating skills to your kids. With your guidance, they can learn how to work out their differences by giving each other the space and independence they so desperately crave. After all, most of the time they're arguing just to see who can get your attention first!

Identify the Problem

The first thing you need to do is stop the misbehaving. If one child is throwing toys or hitting the other, then step in and make it clear that this is unacceptable behavior. Next, ask them to describe what the problem is. Since they'll both want to speak first, you'll need to call on one to go first and let the other one know he can go first next time. After each child explains his side of the story, repeat what each one said and ask if you understood it correctly. Once they agree with you, ask them, one at a time, if they understand the other one's problem.

You'll usually get a "Yeah, but . . ." answer to this question, so be ready to jump in and prevent any statements that will antagonize the other child. You're trying to teach them how to remain calm and deal with one issue at a time.

By reiterating their problems individually, you're letting them know that you understand them and know what they want. Asking them to openly recognize the other sibling's problem gives them the opportunity to understand what happened to make everybody so upset.

This first step is an important one because it teaches your children how to let go of the anger they feel for the other person in the argument. It also teaches them how to communicate effectively so others will understand them. Another thing they learn from this step is that you will always be willing to give them the floor and allow them to tell their own side of the story. Because they know you will listen to them, they will be more likely to go to you with problems.

Find Solutions

Once the problems are out in the open, the next step is to actively engage the siblings in the process of coming up with solutions. Start off by giving your suggestion in the form of a "What if" question, then ask each child for an idea on how to fix the problem. Acknowledge their answers with positive statements like, "That's good" or "We can certainly give that a try" so they feel like they're not always giving the wrong answers. Keep exchanging ideas until all of you can agree on the best one and restate the final solution so both siblings are clear on what needs to happen. For example, "Jimmy will use the computer for one hour after school while Tommy does his homework, then Tommy will use the computer for one hour after dinner while Jimmy does his homework."

Establishing a Set of Rules

Depending on what the siblings are arguing over, a set of rules will help prevent future disagreements about the same issue. For example, if they're fighting over who gets to take the dog out for a walk before dinner, create a schedule in which they each get to do it every other day. If an argument gets violent, establish a rule in which both siblings will be punished no matter who hit first.

In addition to setting rules, let your children know that they can always go to you when they're experiencing problems that they can't solve on their own. Eventually, they'll learn how to handle their own disputes and work out the issues for themselves.

Dealing with Homework

The best negotiating skill you can apply here is setting an agenda and teaching your children how to stick to it. Designate a specific time and place in the house for your children to do their homework every night. The time right before or right after dinner is usually favored because they will have had plenty of time to unwind and play with friends after school. If necessary, meet with teachers ahead of time to find out the types of assignments being handed out and the average time that each student should expect to spend on homework.

Choose a place that's easy for your children to see you in case they have questions; the kitchen table or the desk in the study provide flat surfaces to write on and plenty of light. You can also give your children a few options or let them come up with some ideas of their own. If they suggest the picnic table outside, explain why this might not work (wind blows papers away, rain gets everything wet) and offer more choices. You also might want to busy yourself with your own work, such as paying bills or opening mail, so your children feel like you're all accomplishing tasks together.

If your children give you a hard time about doing their homework, offer to go through it with them, but make sure they know they have to do the work themselves. If they get distracted and start asking for snacks or toys, tell them you'll think about fixing a snack when the homework is finished, and provide something to drink instead.

One way to motivate your children to do their homework is to set up a workstation complete with all the school supplies they'll ever need: pencils, pens, markers, crayons, scissors, glue stick, stapler, and plenty of paper. If you have room, create a little area for them in the study so they feel they have their own space. However, monitor their work so they don't lose focus by playing with all the supplies you've put out for them.

Kid Responsibilities—Chores

The role that chores play in your child's life is a necessary one. Doing chores teaches responsibility, builds self-esteem and self-reliance, and allows the child to feel important.

FACT

Children are able to help at a very early age, and it should be encouraged as soon as they're capable. Otherwise, the older they are when you begin giving them chores, the harder it is to get them to cooperate.

Be sure you assign chores that are appropriate to your child's age. Young children love pitching in around the house because it makes them feel "all grown up" and proud of themselves for doing a great job. However, the older they get, the less eager they are about doing chores because they'd rather spend their time playing with toys or hanging out with friends.

Most experts agree that giving an allowance for chores is not a good idea because it weakens the importance of getting the chores done. If children believe that they should receive money every time they do something around the house, they'll be more likely to rebel against doing the chore and less likely to do things around the house without being asked or given money. They're also denied the chance to understand the significance of taking care of themselves and their home. On the other hand, a lot of parents believe that giving an allowance for chores provides children with an incentive for doing the work. While it's ultimately up to you to decide what works best for your family, there are many imaginative ways to involve them in housework.

Be Creative with Preschoolers

Toddlers love to be called upon to do any task you throw their way. Their curious little minds are always looking for the next engaging activity and the next opportunity to show mom and dad how smart they are. For this reason, you can turn any small task into a big deal for your child. Reserve a little extra time in the morning, and ask your children if they can dress themselves that day. You can even let them choose their outfits, adding even more importance to the task.

At this age, children are also capable of picking up their own clothes and putting them in the laundry basket. Make the chore fun by taking a trip to the store with your child to pick a special basket just for this use. Bright colors and lovable animals always win children over.

You can teach organization skills by having children keep their books stacked neatly, their toys put away, and their beds made. Occasionally leave little surprises on the bookshelf, in the toy box, or under the pillow to encourage your child to continue doing the tasks.

Use a Task Board for Grade-Schoolers

Since children who are in grade school have more responsibilities (homework, extracurricular activities), they're not as interested in taking out the trash, feeding the dog, or setting the table as they are in playing a video game or riding their bikes. Because there's a lot to occupy their minds, they often forget to do chores or just brush them off as useless or boring. One way to keep your children focused on the importance of their duties at home is to set up a task board in a place where they'll be sure to see it, such as the kitchen. You can use the gold star system on a board you make yourself, or you can purchase one from a store. There are many different types available. Some have themes with popular cartoon or movie characters, making it more appealing for the child to check the board.

ALERT!

Using a task board is one way to keep your children on schedule, but employ a method that works best for your family. Your goal is to get them to check the schedule and perform the duties required of them for that day. Make sure you write in your own chores so they can see how everyone in the family has a responsibility.

If your son loves math, you can challenge him with a question for each chore. For example, if his job is to take out the trash, ask him to measure the distance between the house and the garbage barrel.

Be Specific with Teenagers

Teenagers can be difficult when it comes to doing chores. Because they're older, their responsibilities are more involved and more time-consuming. They don't want to spend an hour washing, drying, and folding the laundry or doing the dishes and vacuuming all the rugs in the house. They want to talk on the phone, go out with their friends, and shop at the mall.

The key to negotiating with your teens is to treat them like adults. This always appeals to teenagers! Draw up a mock contract and explain how you're going to use it to bind the agreement that the two of you will make.

Next, sit down to discuss and negotiate terms, concessions, and consequences of breaking the contract, settle on a final agreement, and create the official contract. Terms can include what chores the teen is responsible for; concessions can be what the teen will be allowed to do if the chore is completed, and consequences can include what privileges the teen will lose if the contract is broken. Adjust the contract as needed to fit your teenagers' lifestyle. For example, if they decide to take on more extracurricular activities or a part-time job, you'll need to come up with a new schedule that allows them to get their chores done as well.

Discussing the Allowance

Granting your child an allowance is a privilege that teaches them many valuable lessons that they will carry into their adult lives. It improves their math skills, teaches them responsibility and the value of saving money, and gives them a basic understanding of how the world works. It also teaches them how to prioritize their wants, set goals to acquire the things they want, and feel a sense of accomplishment when a goal is reached. Because there are so many things they want you to buy for them (toys, snacks, games), it's important to involve them in financial processes. Doing so helps them understand why you can't buy them everything their hearts desire. An allowance also serves as a useful negotiating tool when they're begging you to buy them "just this one thing and I won't ask for anything else ever again."

When you make the decision to give children their own money, you also need to teach them how to use it. Explain to them where you get your money and how you manage it. Tell them what a budget is, and show them how you balance your checkbook. You can explain it in simple terms that they'll understand and give them examples of how they can start using their money in some of the same ways. The sooner they begin to understand the concept, the sooner they'll understand how negotiating works.

Let's say there's a video game your daughter is really anxious to get, but it costs so much money that she wouldn't be able to get it until she saved her allowance for ten months. Use this opportunity to give her choices and explain the pros and cons of each one. If she borrowed the money from you, she'd have to go ten months without an allowance to pay you back.

What if there were other things she wanted between now and then? How would she feel if her friends invited her to go for ice cream, but she didn't have the money to go? Give her the option of doing extra chores to earn a little more money. After you discuss different money concepts and provide various options, she may discover that the video game isn't as important as she thought.

Snack Time

Kids love snacks as much as they love toys. That said, it's just as important to teach them the benefits of good nutrition as it is to teach them how to use money wisely to get the things they want. To begin with, it's not always a good idea to use snacks as a means of rewarding your children. They'll have a hard time learning how to pay attention to their bodies and how to recognize when they're hungry as opposed to when they just want something sweet.

ALERT!

Another disadvantage to rewarding your children with snacks is that they will begin to associate emotion (happiness) with food, a dangerous thought process that, if not controlled, often leads to one of the nation's leading epidemics—obesity.

Your children learn from your eating habits, so the best way to teach them about eating healthy is to involve them in the preparation of food. When they ask you for a snack, offer them a creative alternative. You can suggest having a cheese-and-cracker picnic in the back yard and let them put the crackers on a plate and stir the iced tea or lemonade. Another idea is to answer their request for a snack by giving them an art project. Choose colorful vegetables, fruits, cheeses, and nuts and show them how to make funny faces or pretty flowers with the ingredients. Make popcorn and experiment with a few different toppings, such as cinnamon or cumin.

Get your children to think differently about food by offering to have pancakes or eggs for dinner instead of the usual. Let them handle the food and help choose the pans or bowls you'll need. Help them understand food so they're not afraid to try new things. You can even try new things together by offering to be the first one to try something (after showing a little apprehension). The more food choices your children have, the less upset they'll be about not having the snack they saw on television.

Chapter 20

The Ripple Effect of Good Negotiating

Good negotiating has the potential to create a win/win situation every time. That's why, whether you're buying a car or working out a vital business deal, it's important to avoid bad negotiating strategies. Beyond the immediate benefit of emerging from a deal satisfied that both you and your opponent got what you wanted, there are long-term, indirect advantages to cultivating a win/win negotiating style.

Building Trust

Before you find yourself in your counterparts' good graces, you must first give them the opportunity to trust you. Once they feel like you're trustworthy, that's it—you're in. Rapport develops more naturally because you've proven that you're not just "in it to win it," you're in it to develop solutions that work. This level of trust can be accomplished by fostering your negotiating relationships every step of the way. Once you've established that trust, it's important to maintain it.

Some people will never trust you. It seems that no matter what lengths you take, they simply do not budge. Maybe they had bad experiences with past negotiations and have trouble letting down their guard. Or maybe it's a front they use to avoid being taken at the negotiating table. Regardless of the reason, don't get discouraged. Continue to present yourself as someone to be trusted. Your counterpart will appreciate your consistency and professionalism.

The best way to gain your counterpart's trust is with actions that demonstrate your reliability and commitment. Just saying "You can trust me" or "I'm an honest person" won't sound very convincing. Worse, some may assume that just the opposite is true. You want the other party to pick up on your sincerity, and this can't happen if you come off too strong by being too eager to make a good impression. Consequently, it will be more difficult for you to work on the relationship if the other person is skeptical about what you say.

Set the Tone

You want the other party to feel comfortable working with you right from the beginning. One way to accomplish this is to be clear that you would like to approach the discussion by brainstorming to find the most effective solutions for both of you. Explain that you feel both of you have much more to gain by working together instead of against each other. If the other party agrees, be sure to show your enthusiasm. If you get resistance, ask for a description of the other party's main goal, and provide the reasons that your approach is the best way to reach it. Because you're not being demanding about how you'd like to conduct the discussion, the other party will surely note your cooperative skills and optimistic outlook.

How you present yourself can make all the difference when you enter the negotiation room. The way you carry yourself says a lot to your counterpart about the attitude you're taking toward the discussion and toward him. When you first see him, present a genuine smile, a firm handshake, and say something nice, like "How was your flight?" or "It's good to see you again."

FACT

People will feel more relaxed if you are open and act friendly. It's also important to get the other person to open up; you can do this by asking encouraging questions. This will demonstrate that you're interested in what he has to say and that you are ready to listen to his concerns.

The atmosphere you create can influence your counterpart in deciding whether to trust you. If you break the ice by being the first one to talk, you'll have the advantage of setting a positive tone. Being in the driver's seat also allows you to get to know the other party a little better because you're in a position to be the first to ask questions. Furthermore, you can direct the conversation and get the agenda underway by asking questions related to specific topics.

Be Approachable

No matter how much knowledge or leverage you have, throwing your weight around will only succeed in distancing your counterpart. Instead, relate to her by showing you are just as much a human being as she is. Express your feelings about any issue or possible outcome you don't agree with, but be sure to stay in control of your emotions, remaining calm and collected. Talk about why something doesn't work for you, and look for common elements that will help you come up with a solution that does. Portraying a positive attitude shows the other party that you're willing to look at problems from every angle in order to get to the bottom of them.

The more you show your counterparts your honest side, the more they'll trust you. Of course, you don't want to give everything away and make yourself a target, but you do want to let them know where you're coming from so they're aware of the challenges you have to face. Giving away this bit of information is also a time-saver because you're able to work around the roadblocks and resolve differences more quickly.

A small gesture can go a long way. You can establish a comfortable atmosphere by "setting the table" with a pitcher of cold water, dishes of candy, or other refreshments.

A positive viewpoint is another element that shows how easy you are to talk to and work with. If you want the other party to let his guard down a little, you'll have to do the same. Laughter is a great way to lighten up the mood in any situation, and it also gets people talking again. If you're stuck on an issue and you both feel you've exhausted every possible angle, find a way to joke about it. You'll instantly begin to loosen up and hopefully be able to move on with the topic you're discussing. Don't be afraid to get dramatic! Stand up, walk over to the window, and say something like, "Aha! The answer to our problem lies somewhere out there in that busy street. Now if only we can find it." This little tension breaker might be all you need to put you back on that road to discovery.

Do What You Say You'll Do

When people say they'll get back to you, isn't it nice when they actually do? A person who lives up to his obligation is the first person you contact for information, even if several other people can easily provide you with it.

Dependable people are incredibly valuable. If your counterpart did not fulfill an obligation to the shipping company, you will have to delay the shipment of products to your customers, making them angry and possibly distrustful of your company's practices. Similarly, you'll begin to distrust your counterpart because of that failure to come through on an acknowledged duty.

ALERT!

Avoid making promises you aren't sure you can keep. If someone asks you a question that you can't answer, say that you'll look into the issue—and really mean it. Each time you make good on a promise, whether big or small, it will be remembered. The more you live up to your end of the deal, the more good things you say about your character.

A Collaborative Effort

Once you and the other party have established trust, you'll have an easier time working together without worrying about being manipulated. With each subsequent negotiation, this trust will grow deeper, and you'll be able to open up to each other even more. As a result, you'll be able to present more realistic ideas and create more effective solutions. Like any good relationship, it takes time to build a solid foundation. It also involves having to work through many struggles, helping each other every step of the way.

Two Heads Are Better Than One

Because we all have so much to offer, it seems natural that we pool our talents to devise as many solutions as possible and choose the one that fits best. Conversely, if one of us holds back, we take something away from the negotiation, and the most reasonable resolution may be overlooked or never found.

A good negotiator knows that the combined knowledge of all parties involved is more useful than that of only one party. This noncompetitive method of negotiating gives everyone the opportunity to voice their opinions, express their thoughts, and make a contribution to the final outcome. You're also more likely to understand each other's struggles and satisfy each other's needs, even if it means having to compromise when a win/win solution just isn't possible.

What you learn from one negotiation could be applied to another one and might be used in a slightly different way. Let's say you're on an interview, and you pick up on the interviewer's strategy for avoiding the discussion of pay scale. You might find that it comes in handy on your next interview.

From this point, you can analyze how and why you both came up with your numbers, moving another step closer to a possible solution. For example, you might discover that your price is a result of gaining almost no profit from the interest rate, while his price takes into account the hefty fees he's required to pay. All of these figures can be adjusted and balanced until they work for both of you. Without the help of brainstorming techniques, you might not have taken a second look at interest rates or fees.

Establishing the Possibilities

Brainstorming is essential when the goal is to discover the answer that will solve both parties' problems. It's a process that allows you to look at old problems in new ways until you find something that works. The way to approach it is to get everything out in the open—ideas, examples, scenarios—and explore each option with more brainstorming. Your idea could spur your counterpart's idea, which will lead you to yet another idea, and so on. Don't stop when you come upon something that works; keep thinking, and let more possibilities enter the mix. When you're finished brainstorming, you should have a slew of possibilities lined up and ready to be investigated.

The next step in the brainstorming process is to go through each suggestion, one by one, and decide on the one that works the best. Because most problems have more than one solution, it's important to let every idea surface, giving each one equal consideration. Sometimes you'll come up with even more ideas while looking at other ones, and those should be deliberated as well.

Once every possibility is exhausted, you and your counterpart will need to find the plan that suits both of your needs. If one of you is hesitant, don't settle for the solution. Instead, work through it until you both agree that it's the best one. Otherwise, the issue might come up again later and delay the closing. If a solution isn't readily apparent, go back and do some more brainstorming until you have another handful of options. Unless the issue is easy to resolve, don't miss out on the opportunity to brainstorm each topic that comes up. This type of creative thinking is an important step in the negotiation because it puts the responsibility of problem-solving on all parties involved rather than on one person.

Putting Ideas into Practice

It's one thing for you and your counterpart to come to an agreement about how to decide on who gets what, but it's an entirely different thing to back up those words with actions. It's always possible that you're dealing with someone who only appears to want to play fair. As concessions begin to be addressed, monitor the other party. Note the number of unfair tactics being used or behaviors displayed that don't fall in step with that of a win/win negotiator. If you have to, clarify again what you're trying to do and how you both agreed to go about it. Once the other party realizes that you have your guard up, the negotiation will hopefully get back on track.

The success that comes from a good negotiation relies heavily on the success of finding the right interpersonal balance between you and the other party. You're bound to have conflicting points of view and opposing interests; handling them shrewdly is vital to your relationship. Win/win negotiating makes this possible. It is the best way to ensure the possibility of future dealings because it avoids creating a dichotomy at the negotiating table. For example, a mentality of strong/weak; better/worse; winner/loser does not exist because each party is considered equal and cooperates on the same level.

Have Fun with It

At the heart of win/win negotiating is the desire to have an enjoyable experience. You might be wondering how in the world a negotiation can possibly be pleasant. Well, it can be—if you let this book guide you toward operating from a win/win frame of mind. The information presented here is your key to unlocking the mystery of what your counterpart needs and wants in your effort to understand both sides of the negotiation as clearly as possible. You already know what your goals are, so it only makes sense to learn about the other party's interests and see how they combine with yours.

FACT

Almost every time you employ this method ("almost" because not all people agree with win/win negotiating), you will be able to walk away with a very positive experience. For this reason, you want to build a future with as many win/win negotiators as possible.

Good listening habits are also critical to your negotiating relationships. Being a good listener not only shows other parties that you are sincere, it encourages them to give you the same respect. Turn off your internal dialogue while your counterpart is speaking. Don't think about how you're going to respond, what you plan to say about a point you want to make, or when you'll be able to make it to the grocery store. Really focus in on what you are being told, especially since the information you're getting might require some reading between the lines.

Ongoing Relationships

Although short-term relationships should be treated respectfully, special attention should be paid to other parties whom you will need to work with again in future negotiations. When a contract ends, you may want to negotiate another, or you may want to modify an existing one.

Once you've been working with someone for a while, you reach a point in which you both feel comfortable enough to make suggestions without worrying about how the other will react to them. It's important to hear each other out when suggesting a change or eliminating an idea altogether. Know that these suggestions are not meant to be offensive, so don't take them personally. When delivered from the appropriate person, this type of constructive criticism is merely another form of brainstorming. The other party is basically telling you which ideas work from that side of the table and which do not.

Your focus should always be on mutual satisfaction with every decision that's made. This is a significant point because it is the one goal that you and your counterpart share; therefore, it acts as the driving force behind every outcome. As with any other relationship, you must be willing to put your feelings out there and express the opinions and ideas you think work best.

Know your settlement range, which should include all possible outcomes from your ideal to the worst-case scenario. Having this range helps you and your counterpart shift the discussion from negotiating to problem-solving. If it's determined that the best possible outcome falls below your ideal but is still above your bottom line, then consider it a win.

Improving Your Skills

You should always come out of a negotiation feeling like you've gained a little more knowledge and a lot more experience. While there are many experts on the subject, no one is beyond learning something new. This is because people are different, circumstances are varied, and business practices and trends change all the time. Fortunately, all these differences mean more experience under your belt.

One way to increase your knowledge is to look at your past negotiations and pick out the things that worked for you and those that didn't. Don't overanalyze the entire discussion. Instead, look for your strengths and weaknesses and learn how they benefited and hurt your strategy. This section covers several techniques for helping yourself become the best negotiator you can be.

Realistic Expectations

It's natural to have a lot of expectations, especially if you're not used to the process. You have your agenda set, your goals and objectives in order, your plan laid out, and your strategy in place. Then the time comes for you to get down to business, and you realize that some things are not what you predicted them to be. You might learn that the other party has an agenda of her own. She's being uncooperative and won't let you get a word in. This is when you learn how to be flexible by adapting to the situation that's presented to you.

Never assume that you know exactly what you're going to get from the other party. Having expectations like these only prevents you from asking questions to learn more about her "real" position. Although it's safe to draw some general conclusions based on the information you've turned up in your research, it's risky to think you've got it all covered.

Unlimited Potential

Because there is always something you can do to improve, you should never stop looking for opportunities to practice your skills. Resources can be found everywhere, whether in books like this one or in line at the department store. As soon as you begin to see the world through a negotiator's eyes, the possibilities for success are limitless. Work on your style, and discover new methods by attending a workshop. Find a mentor to help you flesh out some ideas, or look at college courses related to negotiating.

The negotiation process is not a science and does not follow a defined set of rules. You have to be able to adapt to many situations if you want to do well. Don't be afraid to try new things, and apply anything you've learned the next time you negotiate. It's better to know whether something works than to forget about it altogether.

Your Report Card of Success

It worked for you when you were in school, so why not use it again? Using a grading system to measure your success is a good way to look back on the negotiation with a positive attitude and look forward to future negotiations with optimism. You don't want to beat yourself up over what you could've and should've done, but you do want to critique your performance by assessing the major points. How well did you prepare? How effective was your style? How quickly were you able to adapt to changes? Would you consider your relationship with the other party a good one?

FACT

Making an assessment allows you to step back and look at your overall presentation with a new perspective. Since the deal is done, you no longer feel the pressure to execute your strategy perfectly. Instead, you can step back and evaluate yourself objectively.

Remember not to be harsh on yourself. You want to feel good about the work you just did; otherwise, you'll only end up regretting your decisions and possibly not following through on your commitments. To conduct the evaluation without shaking your confidence in your abilities, look for things that need to be further developed. For example, make a note to work on your listening skills and remind yourself to ask more questions. Don't forget to celebrate the things that worked well for you. Your ability to make the other party feel comfortable with you is a huge victory.

Getting All A's

Remember how great you felt when you got your report card and it was sprinkled with A's? You were so proud of yourself that you couldn't wait to run home to show it to your parents. Relive that moment of pride by putting together a report card that reflects a job-well-done in the working world. The following list illustrates the most important points of negotiating, so give yourself an A for each one you were able to attain:

- ☐ Assembled the appropriate amount of information
- ☐ Achieved objectives and goals
- ☐ Acquired new skills
- ☐ Advanced relationship with other negotiators
- ☐ Accomplished win/win solutions

As you can see, these A's are certainly something to feel good about. Put them on a sheet of paper so you can hang it on your refrigerator as a constant reminder of what you are capable of achieving.

One F Is Good

Who says all Fs have to be bad? There is one F that you can feel good about putting on your perfect report card because it doesn't stand for "fail." On the contrary, the F on your report card is for Fulfillment—the overall satisfaction of doing the best job possible. Fulfillment comes from knowing and feeling that the time you invested in something paid off; you did everything you set out to do and walked away with dignity. It also stems from self-respect (standing up for yourself when you have to) and consideration for others (helping your counterpart achieve his goals). So in addition to all those well-deserved A's, go ahead and give yourself an F!

Enjoying the Ride

A good negotiation will leave you surprised at how much enjoyment you receive from it. Not only do you get the opportunity to achieve your goals, you get to work with (and learn from) some very talented and skilled people. Together, you and your counterpart embark on a journey of discovery and creativity in which the perfect plan is developed. Along the way, you engage in thought-provoking discussions that invigorate the mind and refresh the pool of ideas that you've amassed. As a result, the bonds you form help lead to agreements and further the possibility of future commitments.

Chapter 21

What Every Successful Negotiator Knows

Whether you're embarking on a career path filled with negotiations or trying to get through a single life-changing event, the skills you learn from this book will remain with you forever. Keep them sharp by using them often, and be willing to learn from every experience. Over time, you'll recognize what works best for you and what brings you the most success. In the meantime, this chapter will tell you what's working for the experts.

"See" the Deal

The ability to dream is a powerful tool in all aspects of life. When it comes to negotiating, it's something that allows you to discover many possibilities. If you envision how the meeting will unfold, you can better prepare for potential situations. If you let your imagination run wild, you can think up all sorts of scenarios and plan how to handle them if they take place. Sparking the creative side of your brain even before the preparation stage gives you the opportunity to get ready for the unexpected by developing a myriad of protective strategies. For instance, if you concoct a hypothetical situation in which your counterpart suddenly brings more team members into the negotiation, you can then put together a plan for countering that move.

Developing a mental picture of what will take place beforehand also gives you the opportunity to analyze the negotiation from all angles, so you can devise a list of questions and gather suitable information. You'll also want to highlight areas where you foresee potential conflicts and figure out ways to prevent them from happening as well as solutions for overcoming them if they do happen.

This preemptive step can end up saving you a lot of time because the solutions you think up can also be used to resolve disputes you're having in other areas of the discussion.

Another way to use your imagination for planning purposes is to come up with probable outcomes of all your and the other party's possible issues. This will help you establish your settlement range (discussed in Chapter 1) because you'll be able to place a level of importance on each possible outcome. It will also help you direct the negotiation toward solution-oriented discussions instead of getting stuck on one issue after another.

Predict Variables

In order to conduct a thorough analysis of the negotiation, take it apart to investigate each of its parts, and then see how many ways you can put it back together. Experiment with the parts by seeing if and how they relate to each other. For example, can you offer the other party a lower shipping fee and make up for it in the cost of installation? Out of all the financial issues, is any one interchangeable and if so, how flexible can you afford to be? How strict are certain deadlines compared to others, and can they be extended? The answers to these questions will provide you with a good overview of what you gain and what you stand to lose with each issue.

You can also use the process as an aid in determining the importance of individual issues. Prioritizing is essential because you'll need to know when you should pick your battles and when you shouldn't. An issue of great importance should never be compromised, and you should be as firm as possible without being demanding. Let the other party know that you cannot bend on certain issues, but also offer a few different suggestions that benefit him as well.

Additionally, back up your position with tangible evidence, such as printed reports or company documents. This lets the other party see first-hand how serious the issue is. It also might encourage him to do the same for you when the time comes.

FACT

When you look at how many different ways the negotiation can unfold, you're able to predict certain outcomes and therefore have the information readily available if you need it.

Prepare for Change

Since the act of negotiation doesn't follow a set pattern, something is inevitably going to change, and you need to be prepared for it. This change could be in the other party's behavior at closing. For example, she suddenly wants to take back most of her concessions because she's having second thoughts. It will then be up to you to point out how she's benefiting from the agreements that were made and why the negotiation should move forward.

Another way change occurs is when a solution you thought was workable suddenly becomes unacceptable because of other agreements that were made. If this happens, you'll have to look at the agreements affecting the change, determine which one is more important, and discuss how it can be reworked to find the best solution. For example, while you're discussing your need to have at least 40 percent of the shipping costs paid for, the other party discovers that the high price agreed upon to pay for installation will make the cost for shipping prohibitive. Clearly, both issues need to be re-evaluated to determine how the costs can be adjusted.

You'll lose a little time because you'll have to go back and renegotiate something that was already settled. However, it's a good idea to reassess your goals because you might feel differently about their priority levels as the discussion moves along.

Have a Walk-away Point

One of the most important things you can bring with you to the table is your walk-away point. Without this, you can negotiate for hours, giving everything away without getting any of your needs met.

ALERT!

To avoid being taken advantage of, let the other party know that you cannot negotiate successfully with him if he does not respect your bottom line. Keep in mind that you can always return another time if the other party agrees to make some changes.

Having a walk-away point gives you leverage; without you, there's no way for the other party to realize any goals. However, use it only when absolutely necessary or else you risk losing the opportunity to devise a mutual solution. Give your counterpart the chance to work with you, and make it clear that you don't want to walk away if you don't have to.

Make Connections

Negotiating is all about making one connection after another. Whether you're looking for creative solutions to difficult problems, reading your counterpart's body language to uncover any hidden agenda, or establishing a positive beginning to a long-term relationship, the connections you make are important indicators of your next move. You should always be looking for ways to put similar and differing elements together to see what you can come up with. Sometimes the most successful solutions are hidden within an obscure combination of elements that you never would have guessed existed.

Think about the relationship you're trying to build with your counterpart. How can you continue to improve it so you both leave the negotiation feeling a sense of partnership? The answer lies in how open you're willing to be. While you never want to lay all your cards out on the table, it is important that you give the other party new information if the situation calls for it. This allows her to see your point more clearly, and it gives her the opportunity to respond with an equal amount of openness. The result? You both learn something fundamental about each other's role in the deal.

QUESTION?

When is it a good time to reveal information?

Usually, if your experience with the other party has been positive, it's in the best interest of the negotiation as a whole to spill the beans. Even if you don't think your information will help, share it anyway. Your counterpart might be able to come up with a few ideas that you haven't thought of, which in turn can lead to the solution that you both have been looking for.

Of Preference or Necessity

It will help if you can distinguish between the other party's needs and wants. This will allow you to make better decisions about how much time you'll spend discussing particular issues. It will also help you determine what concessions you're willing to make and how flexible you'll be when making them.

One way to separate needs from wants is to explore how many possible outcomes there are per subject. Because needs are more complex and sometimes contingent on other things, they produce the most satisfactory outcomes. Wants, on the other hand, are usually specific requests that cannot be satisfied in more than a few ways. They're usually things like free warranties, an extra shipment of goods, extended services, or some other kind of perk.

ALERT!

When making concessions, be sure that the other party gives value for value and doesn't try to offer a small concession in return for an important one. Be fair, and maintain equilibrium by always trading big items for big items and small for small.

If the other party hasn't been upfront about his needs and wants, ask questions to get that information for yourself. Do some creative thinking by providing examples of benefits that might be possible if you had enough information to go on. You could say, "If your biggest concern is price, we can knock off 5 percent here and pick it up on the shipping end. But if you're more concerned with the deadline, then we can get the products to you thirty days early and charge full price." Pay attention to what is most interesting, and come up with more solutions to that problem.

Have an Open Mind

When we find a system that works, we tend to use it over and over and over again. Similarly, when we find a negotiating style we're comfortable with, we use it every chance we get. But all successful negotiators know how important it is to tailor their style to match the other party's behavior. If your style involves analyzing every detail and your counterpart's is to be more direct, it's a good idea to summarize your findings rather than discussing every element. If you and the other party are equally skilled negotiators, you will both be making the same effort to adapt to each other's needs.

As long as you remember that all negotiators have their own way of doing things and nobody is right or wrong, then you can make it in any negotiation. The importance of being open-minded is especially apparent during the bargaining phase, in which everyone tries to find the best way to reach agreements. When the negotiation reaches that point, be respectful to everyone's ideas, and seriously think about each one. Be honest about whether you think something works, and give explanations for why you feel the way you do.

FACT

An exchange of ideas may spawn a lot of new possibilities that can put a refreshing twist on the problem you're trying to solve. Don't be quick to reject these new ideas because you never know where they're going to lead you. Explore each one and continue to let the ideas flow until—eureka!—you find the right one.

Just as we all have a different negotiating style, we also have our own way of problem-solving, communicating, and making decisions. Before you immediately snub their practices, try to learn something from them. Above all, don't try to force your systems on them; they'll only feel like you're being critical.

Create an Atmosphere of Respect

Successful negotiators understand the importance of working in an atmosphere that's comfortable and conflict-free. They also know that while some level of stress is to be expected, creating more stress on top of that is unnecessary. For this reason, they don't behave irrationally by insulting the other party, and they use their best listening skills. Additionally, they remain firm with the issues that are important to them while remaining calm and unemotional.

A negotiator of this caliber knows that if you are a professional, you need to act like one. They instinctively know what the other party is thinking, and just to be sure, they ask questions that show their willingness to learn more about the other party's objectives. Just thinking about negotiating in this kind of atmosphere is enough to produce a calm effect!

By now, you must be wondering how these exceptional negotiators learned to be so proficient at what they do. Among their many skills, one of the most important is that they understand human nature. They know that some people can't control their emotions when faced with tough decisions; that people change their minds on a whim; that it's in our genes to become aggressive when we're not getting our way. Throughout all of these challenges, the successful negotiator never loses her cool, never takes it personally, and never stops pushing to reach a jointly designed win/win outcome.

Handle Power Appropriately

Power itself is not a negative thing to possess; rather, it's how people sometimes misuse power that gives it a bad reputation. Using it to control other people is unethical and one-sided, while using it to produce a positive result is productive. Sometimes people have the power to make changes, but they don't use it because they're either unaware that they have it or they just don't make the effort.

Though some negotiators believe that there is always one person who has more power than the other, the opposite is actually true. If someone did hold all the power, why would they need the other person to help them achieve their goals? In fact, you should never underestimate how strong the other party actually is, because their strength may show up in unexpected ways.

Make Good Use of Time

Good negotiators use time wisely by conducting each step with efficiency. They don't promote situations that include offering and counteroffering back and forth for extended periods. They know that only one offer at a time should be up for discussion. If the other party continues to ignore your offer by coming up with his own, start asking him questions that bring his attention back to yours. If he still continues to negotiate this way, get up, gather your belongings, and leave.

Play Fair

In order for you as a negotiator to set the stage for success and gain respect from your counterpart, you must use win/win negotiation strategies every step of the way. When people enter into a negotiation, they expect to be treated as if their needs were not that important. What they don't expect is the very thing that you should give them—star treatment. When you demonstrate that your counterpart's needs are important to the success of your goals, you'll gain immediate respect.

Being fair involves treating your counterpart as a friend of the family—with courtesy, politeness, and warmth. Avoid putting the other party in uncomfortable situations by using pressure tactics or emotional ploys to get your way.

Stick to your goals, but be kind about it; question ideas, but don't criticize; be yourself, but be considerate of your counterpart's personality; keep discussions moving forward, but don't rush through the issues; encourage new ideas, but take them seriously. Every successful negotiator knows that ruthlessness will get you nowhere fast.

Communicate Well

If you think about it, we should all be experts on communication—we have so many ways of doing it: telephone, television, newspapers, books, Internet, snail mail, art, music, and so on. However, when we get together to discuss big issues face to face, some of us have a hard time conveying the right things at the right time.

A good negotiator knows this skill like he was born with it, and he uses it with the same amount of ease he has when talking to his best friend. Luckily, for those who are lacking in the communication department, there are plenty of books, classes, workshops, seminars, self-help CDs, and Web sites to get information from and use for improvement. Take advantage of these tools because you won't be able to live without them.

Self-Confidence Is Key

Master negotiators are comfortable no matter where they negotiate, what they negotiate, or whom they negotiate with. They know that in order to get their message across, they have to be confident enough to make enthusiastic presentations about their ideas as well as argue their needs with the use of well-prepared facts. Every interaction they have with a counterpart has a purpose, whether it's to convey an idea, discuss an issue, examine a possible solution, or learn something.

They also know screaming and threatening does not make things any better. The only purpose this type of interaction serves is to instill fear in the other person, at which point the exchange of information and ideas is cut off altogether. The successful negotiator knows that the best way to be firm about something is to use tone of voice and a careful choice of words to illustrate a point.

FACT

If you ever find yourself in a position where you and your counterpart just don't seem to be communicating in a way that you can understand each other, pick an issue you want to discuss and write the three most important things about it on a piece of paper. Have your counterpart do the same, and then exchange papers. This may seem silly at first, but it will stimulate your brain and hopefully encourage better communication.

Listen with Conviction

Part of what helps you develop excellent communication skills is having excellent listening skills. This requires more than just hearing what's coming out of the other party's mouth. Actively participate in absorbing the information you're given. Nod your agreement to important points, and write down questions that you want to ask when the presentation is finished.

Let the other party have the floor without interruption. This technique is a good relationship builder because it shows you're genuinely interested in learning. Take notes so you can ask for explanations of anything you didn't understand, and express your eagerness about some of the ideas.

Never Sell Yourself Short

In order to get what you want, you need to ask for it. As obvious as that concept may seem, it's easy to forget when you're trying to build your strategy. You might be too intimidated to ask for more than what you really need because you don't want to offend the other party and risk losing something important. Skilled negotiators are never afraid to ask for something, even if they already have a mile-long wish list. They know that it never hurts to ask and that it's better to get a bunch of negative responses than to wonder later about whether you could have gotten what you didn't ask for.

Once the contract is signed, you won't have another chance to ask for anything. So make sure you write everything down, and ask away.

If you're still worried that you might be asking for more than you should, make a separate list of concessions that you can offer in case the other party gets frustrated with all your requests. Think of concessions that won't hurt that much to give up but that might mean a lot from the receiving end.

Your aspirations determine how satisfied you will be with the outcome of the negotiation. Even if a win/win resolution has been achieved, there's still the possibility of feeling like you didn't get quite what you wanted. The reason for this is that you didn't set your goals high enough, possibly because you felt you were being fair to the other party and saving face in the relationship. A good negotiator realizes that it's a lot tougher to upgrade a goal that was set too low once it's out in the open than it is to lower a goal that started off high. The same holds true if you're a seller and you don't set the price high enough in the beginning. While you want to set a reasonable price, you also want to give yourself enough room to counter the other party's offer.

It's important to have confidence in your goals and to set a bottom line for each one. Know exactly what you want and how far you're willing to go to get it, and you can't get taken advantage of. Use research as your most powerful tool when determining price, especially for big-ticket items such as a car or house. Doing so will give you even more confidence because you can justify your bottom line with tangible proof.

If you want to buy a house with a list price of $320,000, and you know comparable houses in the area have sold for $300,000, you can afford to make a low offer of $295,000—you have evidence to back up your decision. Even though you both know you won't get your asking prices, setting your goals high (which in this case means starting with an offer that's low!) gives you the room to negotiate a price that's fair.

Why Some Negotiations Fail

Aside from knowing what needs to happen to have a successful negotiation, good negotiators know why they sometimes fail. Recognizing and studying these failures is an important part of the learning process and will help you focus on which areas need improvement and which ones are working well. Because experience is the best teacher, it takes time, patience, and perseverance to acquire and develop the skills needed to become a successful negotiator.

Inadequate Preparation

If you don't make the effort to adequately prepare for every step of the negotiation process, you're least likely to achieve a satisfactory outcome. This is the first and most crucial phase in the process. Each one of your arguments will be based on the information you turn up during your research. Even if you spend weeks doing research, you must have the right information, or you risk being caught off guard by the other party. Here are a few knowledge gaps that are evidence of poor planning:

- Lack of information
- No plan for an opening
- No bottom line
- Inaccurate facts
- Bad or no organization skills
- Unorganized agenda
- Vague in the details (dates, prices, quantities)
- Not enough information about the other party

To be sure you're prepared, make a list of the points you need to research. Since this step is the most important one, make sure you give yourself plenty of time. Double-check factual information, and find the answers to every question you have.

Poor Communication

The biggest barrier that prevents you from achieving success often relates to communication. When communication goes bad, everything else follows suit.

FACT

Negotiating is all about exchanging ideas and interacting with the other party. When something inhibits the process, it's very difficult to find solutions to the problems you're facing.

If you and the other party don't seem to be communicating in a way that's beneficial to the discussion, the best thing you can do to clear the air is to say, "I don't feel like we're communicating very well." Work together to pinpoint the problem before you go any further. The following list will help you recognize some of these problems:

- A level of trust hasn't been established.
- One person is dominating every conversation.
- The other party does not have authority to make decisions.
- Disagreements are taken too personally.

- Creative thinking, brainstorming and problem-solving is not taking place.
- Body language is not being observed.
- No one is asking questions.
- Only one side is making concessions.
- Irrational, hostile, and/or abusive behavior is displayed.
- The other party does not know how to negotiate.
- Someone has a negative outlook.

Any kind of mistreatment will hinder the injured party's desire to communicate. Respect and trust are two of the most important factors in conducting a professional discussion. Without them, suspicion remains constant throughout the negotiation, and you will never feel comfortable with what the other party is saying.

Too Many Mistakes

No mistake is small, but when one is made, it's not the end of the world. It's almost necessary to make these mistakes so we can learn from the consequences they produce and avoid making them next time. Even if you feel you didn't make any mistakes with a particular negotiation, look for mistakes your counterpart might have made and learn from those. The following highlights some of the most common oversights:

- Acceptance of the first offer
- Lack of focus
- Inability to adapt to other person's style
- Inflexibility
- Forgetting about one's goals
- Becoming too emotional

Take your time, and be sure you feel comfortable about every decision that's made before moving on to the next issue. Keep moving toward the close, and be attentive to the other party's objectives as well as your own.

Quick-Reference Checklists

This section contains some of the major points that were covered in this book, compiled into convenient checklists that you can easily review any time you need to. They also come in handy if you want to make sure you've covered all your bases before entering into a negotiation. If it helps, make a copy of the pages and keep them with you throughout the entire process so you always have a quick reference guide by your side.

Before You Negotiate

- ☐ Define your main goal.

- ☐ Prioritize the rest of your goals.

- ☐ Decide on the concessions you're willing to make.

- ☐ Define your bottom line.

- ☐ Research your counterpart.

- ☐ Highlight your common goals, and note differences.

- ☐ Gather as much information as possible.

- ☐ Have alternatives.

- ☐ Devise a strategy for a win/win outcome.

- ☐ Create an agenda.

- ☐ Choose a meeting spot.

While You Negotiate

- ☐ Compare your agenda with the other party's agenda.

- ☐ Agree on conducting a win/win discussion.

- ☐ Listen attentively to your counterpart's needs.

- ☐ Verify that he or she has authority to make decisions.

- ☐ Bargain concession for concession.

- ☐ Pay attention to body language.

- ☐ Brainstorm to find the best solution.

- ☐ Make your bottom line known at the right time.

- ☐ Reveal that you have alternatives.

- ☐ Make decisions that move toward closing.

Ending the Negotiation

- ☐ Take a break before closing.

- ☐ Review and confirm every agreement.

- ☐ Avoid making and agreeing to last-minute concessions.

- ☐ Encourage your counterpart to end the deal.

- ☐ Point out the benefits of each agreement.

- ☐ Read the contract carefully.

- ☐ Ask questions about anything you don't understand.

- ☐ Sign and date changes that are made to the contract.

- ☐ Make a list of deadlines to follow up on.

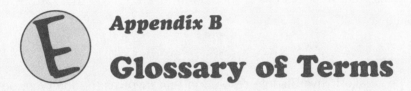

Appendix B

Glossary of Terms

Because there's so much to keep in mind when negotiating and preparing to negotiate, it's easy to forget simple definitions. Use this glossary as a quick reference to keep everything straight.

Add-on

A small concession that a party asks for by adding it to a larger concession that's already been discussed.

Alternative dispute resolution

A process that includes either mediation or arbitration that parties use to avoid a lawsuit.

Arbitration

A type of alternative dispute resolution that involves the intervention of a third party, an arbitrator. The arbitrator directs a hearing and decides who gets what.

Back-end profits

Add-ons usually sold by the financing manager of a car dealership, including extended warranties, rust protection, fabric protection, special painting, and so on.

Bad faith

When a party makes concessions with no intention of fulfilling them.

Bargaining

Discussing the terms of a sale until an agreement is made.

Barter

An exchange of goods or services without the use of money.

Body language

Nonverbal cues that give some indication about what a party is really thinking.

Bogey

A tactic that involves using a scapegoat to explain why you cannot be flexible about an issue.

Boilerplate or form contract

A template that some companies use as their basic contract for every client; lists the conditions and limitations of the agreement.

Bottom line

The point in which the deal is no longer negotiable; your walk-away point.

Breach of contract

When a party does something that goes against a signed contract; failing to perform duties; refusing to do what's expected.

Bundling

When one party gets the other party to make two or more concessions at once by grouping them together so they seem contingent upon each other.

Cadence

The rhythm or style of your voice.

Cap cost

When leasing a car, the price that is equal to the selling price of a car.

Cap cost reduction

The discount car dealerships give off the list price.

Concession

A privilege that's given to the other party in exchange for something else.

Consequential and incidental damages

Money awarded by the court to the injured party for losses that were predicted if a breach of contract occurred.

Consideration

A term for benefits, gains, promises, or services rendered.

Cowry

The thick, glossy shells of marine snails; the first objects to be used as money; longest-used currency in history.

Crunch

A tactic that involves disagreeing with every offer a party makes in an attempt to get them to doubt their position.

Customer rebates

Money that's given to the customer by the manufacturer.

Decoy

Something that is used to divert attention away from the real issue.

Delay tactic

A tactic that is used to stall a negotiation or to gain more time than is probably needed.

Devil's advocate

A training technique in which a person tests your arguments by systematically rejecting everything you offer so you can see all the possible things that could go wrong and devise ways of handling them.

Escalation

A tactic in which you have enough leverage to get more out of a deal than what has already been agreed upon.

Factory-to-dealer cash payments

Payments made to car dealers when certain cars are sold at certain times.

Failure of consideration

When a party does not hold up to its agreed part of the contract.

Fighting Chance

A customer information service that gives you access to automobile industry information. (Call 1-800-288-1134 for more information, or visit the Web at *www.fightingchance.com*).

Flinching

A tactic that involves making an outrageous offer to test the other party's reaction.

Fraud

An intentional act in which a party presents false information to a counterpart, causing them to suffer one or many losses.

Front-end profits

The amount of profit made from the sale of a car; pays sales commission.

Funny money

Something that is used to replace real money so as to shift your focus away from cost or price. Poker chips and percentages are funny money.

Good faith

The implication that everyone will be fair and truthful in order to satisfy the purpose of the negotiation.

Good guy/bad guy tactic

An act in which one person pretends to be difficult, aggressive, and unyielding, while another person on the same negotiating team pretends to be on your side.

High-pressure tactic

A tactic that forces you to make rash decisions out of fear of losing out on the deal altogether.

Hold-back

A portion of the invoice price of a car that the factory holds back and refunds to the dealer when cars are sold.

Imaginary deadline
A proposed deadline that is not real; usually invoked to gain more time.

Invoice price
The actual price of a car as seen on the factory invoice that's billed to the dealer.

Leverage
Something (information, experience, options) that gives a party more of an advantage.

List price
Manufacturer's suggested retail price (MSRP) of a car.

Lose/lose negotiating
When neither party achieves desired goals due to stubborn, uncompromising behavior.

Lowballing
A tactic in which an offer lower than the norm is made.

Market conditions
The current climate for making a certain type of purchase or other negotiation. When buying a house, for instance, market conditions include determining whether you're in a seller's or buyer's market (supply vs. demand), whether interest rates are high or low, and what the home sale trends are.

Market value
The price you can expect for the item you hope to buy or sell. In the case of real estate, often determined by what other houses sold for in the neighborhood you're looking to buy in.

Mediation
A type of alternative dispute resolution that involves the intervention of a third party, a mediator, to help parties resolve issues.

Misrepresentation

When a party unintentionally or intentionally makes false claims.

Money factor

The fee a car dealership charges you for leasing or renting a car.

Nibbling

When a party asks for "one more thing" after an agreement has already been reached.

One-time-only offer

A high-pressure tactic in which a party will pretend that an offer is only good for that day.

Pitch

A high- or low-frequency sound; one of the elements that make up tone.

Playing dumb

A tactic in which a party pretends to be unprepared or uninformed about the subject under discussion in order to acquire information about the other party.

Positional or win/lose negotiating

One party reaches desired goals at the expense of the other party.

Red herring

The process in which a party purposely makes an unrealistic demand so when it's rejected, the thing that's truly desired doesn't seem to be so outrageous.

Release

When a party relinquishes claims, actions, and/or any rights against another party, freeing them of any responsibilities that were stated in an agreement.

Settlement range
The spectrum of possible outcomes between your ideal and worst-case scenarios.

Shill
A person or sales pitch that acts as bait to lure potential customers into the store or onto the car lot, for example.

Socratic method
A tactic that involves asking a series of leading questions in order to manipulate the other person into giving a particular response; based on the technique of the Greek philosopher Socrates, who asked questions in an effort to teach students how to think logically.

Specific performance
A court order that states the offending party must carry out the duties he was under contract to perform instead of (and sometimes in addition to) paying damages.

Splitting the difference
A tactic that involves taking your offer and the other party's offer and settling on the difference between the two numbers.

Stonewalling
A ploy purposely used to draw a party's attention away from the subject at hand.

Straw man tactic
Making the other party believe something is valuable to you when it isn't.

Stress
The emphasis that is placed on words; one of the elements that make up tone.

Tempo
Describes how fast or slow you speak.

Tone
The particular sound given to words to convey a specific meaning; composed of pitch, stress, and volume.

Tort
A civil wrongdoing, such as an intentional physical action (such as a punch or kick) or unintentional act (accidentally injuring someone) that requires a remedy from the court.

Volume
The level of loudness given to words; one of the elements that make up tone.

Web conferencing
Using a company's services to host or participate in meetings via the Internet.

Wholesale value
The value of a car (your trade-in) to someone (dealership) who will resell it for a profit.

Win/win negotiating
Both parties work together to achieve an outcome that is fair and mutually satisfying.

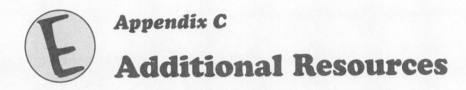

Appendix C

Additional Resources

You've got the basics down, but if you want to continue educating your-self about particular aspects of negotiat-ing, there's a lot of information available to you. This appendix includes suggestions for books and Web sites that may be beneficial to beginning negotiators.

Further Reading

Elliston, Bob. *What Car Dealers Won't Tell You: The Insider's Guide to Buying and Leasing a New or Used Car* (Plume: 1996).

Margulies, Sam, Ph.D., J.D. *Getting Divorced Without Ruining Your Life* (Simon & Schuster: 2001).

Ordway, Nicholas. *The Absolute Beginner's Guide to Buying a House* (Prima Publishing: 2002).

Schapiro, Nicole. *Negotiating for Your Life; New Success Strategies for Women* (Henry Holt and Company, Inc.: 1993).

Ury, William. *Getting Past No: Negotiating with Difficult People* (Bantam Books: 1991).

Woolf, Bob. *Friendly Persuasion: My Life As a Negotiator* (G.P. Putnam's Sons: 1990).

Web Sites

General

Negotiator Magazine

Articles on a variety of topics.w
www.negotiatormagazine.com

Entrepreneur

Covers a variety of business topics and allows you to conduct a search for articles on negotiating.
www.entrepreneur.com

The Wise Negotiator

A newsletter containing articles on negotiating.

✑*www.negotiators.com*

Roger Dawson's Power Negotiating Institute

One of the industry's leading business speakers and authors.

✑*www.rdawson.com*

Everyone Negotiates

A great resource for learning and sharpening skills.

✑*www.everyonenegotiates.com*

Contract Law and Printable Documents

Nolo.com

Law explained in terms the rest of us can understand.

✑*www.nolo.com*

Legaldocs

Legal, printable documents.

✑*www.legaldocs.com*

Free Advice

Legal advice on a variety of topics.

✑*www.freeadvice.com*

Find Law

A place to find a lawyer in your city, printable forms, product recalls, and more.

✑*www.findlaw.com*

Salary Negotiations

JobStar Central

Job search guide with tons of articles on negotiating salary.
✎*www.jobstar.org*

Yahoo! Hot Jobs

Links to a variety of salary resources.
✎*www.hotjobs.com*

Salary.com

Provides an easy-to-use salary wizard.
✎*www.salary.com*

Salary Expert

Offers individual and executive salary reports.
✎*www.salaryexpert.com*

Seminars and Workshops on Negotiating

Negotiation Workshops

✎*www.negotiationsworkshops.com*

Sales Training America

✎*www.salestrainingamerica.com*

Tutorial USA (online training)

✎*www.tutorialusa.com*

Dr. Chester L. Karrass

✎*www.karrass.com*

Other Useful Sites

Advanced Public Speaking Institute

Contains hundreds of articles on the subject of negotiation.

✍*www.public-speaking.org*

Career Journal

The Wall Street Journal's executive career site.

✍*www.careerjournal.com*

Webex

Offers web conferencing tools.

✍*www.webex.com*

Federal Trade Commission

Provides an explanation of the Cooling-off Rule, along with other consumer information.

✍*www.ftc.gov*

Flea Market Guide of U.S. Flea Markets

Allows you to search for flea markets by state.

✍*www.fleamarketguide.com*

 **Index**

THE EVERYTHING SERIES!

BUSINESS

Everything® Business Planning Book
Everything® Coaching and Mentoring Book
Everything® Fundraising Book
Everything® Home-Based Business Book
Everything® Landlording Book
Everything® Leadership Book
Everything® Managing People Book
Everything® Negotiating Book
Everything® Online Business Book
Everything® Project Management Book
Everything® Robert's Rules Book, $7.95
Everything® Selling Book
Everything® Start Your Own Business Book
Everything® Time Management Book

COMPUTERS

Everything® Computer Book

COOKBOOKS

Everything® Barbecue Cookbook
Everything® Bartender's Book, $9.95
Everything® Chinese Cookbook
Everything® Chocolate Cookbook
Everything® Cookbook
Everything® Dessert Cookbook
Everything® Diabetes Cookbook
Everything® Fondue Cookbook
Everything® Grilling Cookbook
Everything® Holiday Cookbook
Everything® Indian Cookbook
Everything® Low-Carb Cookbook
Everything® Low-Fat High-Flavor Cookbook
Everything® Low-Salt Cookbook
Everything® Mediterranean Cookbook
Everything® Mexican Cookbook
Everything® One-Pot Cookbook
Everything® Pasta Cookbook
Everything® Quick Meals Cookbook
Everything® Slow Cooker Cookbook
Everything® Soup Cookbook

Everything® Thai Cookbook
Everything® Vegetarian Cookbook
Everything® Wine Book

HEALTH

Everything® Alzheimer's Book
Everything® Anti-Aging Book
Everything® Diabetes Book
Everything® Dieting Book
Everything® Hypnosis Book
Everything® Low Cholesterol Book
Everything® Massage Book
Everything® Menopause Book
Everything® Nutrition Book
Everything® Reflexology Book
Everything® Reiki Book
Everything® Stress Management Book
Everything® Vitamins, Minerals, and
 Nutritional Supplements Book

HISTORY

Everything® American Government Book
Everything® American History Book
Everything® Civil War Book
Everything® Irish History & Heritage Book
Everything® Mafia Book
Everything® Middle East Book

HOBBIES & GAMES

Everything® Bridge Book
Everything® Candlemaking Book
Everything® Card Games Book
Everything® Cartooning Book
Everything® Casino Gambling Book, 2nd Ed.
Everything® Chess Basics Book
Everything® Crossword and Puzzle Book
Everything® Crossword Challenge Book
Everything® Drawing Book
Everything® Digital Photography Book
Everything® Easy Crosswords Book
Everything® Family Tree Book

Everything® Games Book
Everything® Knitting Book
Everything® Magic Book
Everything® Motorcycle Book
Everything® Online Genealogy Book
Everything® Photography Book
Everything® Poker Strategy Book
Everything® Pool & Billiards Book
Everything® Quilting Book
Everything® Scrapbooking Book
Everything® Sewing Book
Everything® Soapmaking Book

HOME IMPROVEMENT

Everything® Feng Shui Book
Everything® Feng Shui Decluttering Book, $9.95
Everything® Fix-It Book
Everything® Homebuilding Book
Everything® Home Decorating Book
Everything® Landscaping Book
Everything® Lawn Care Book
Everything® Organize Your Home Book

EVERYTHING® KIDS' BOOKS

All titles are $6.95

Everything® Kids' Baseball Book, 3rd Ed.
Everything® Kids' Bible Trivia Book
Everything® Kids' Bugs Book
Everything® Kids' Christmas Puzzle
 & Activity Book
Everything® Kids' Cookbook
Everything® Kids' Halloween Puzzle
 & Activity Book
Everything® Kids' Hidden Pictures Book
 Everything® Kids' Joke Book
Everything® Kids' Knock Knock Book
Everything® Kids' Math Puzzles Book
Everything® Kids' Mazes Book
Everything® Kids' Money Book

All Everything® books are priced at $12.95 or $14.95, unless otherwise stated. Prices subject to change without notice.

Everything® Kids' Monsters Book
Everything® Kids' Nature Book
Everything® Kids' Puzzle Book
Everything® Kids' Riddles & Brain Teasers Book
Everything® Kids' Science Experiments Book
Everything® Kids' Soccer Book
Everything® Kids' Travel Activity Book

KIDS' STORY BOOKS

Everything® Bedtime Story Book
Everything® Bible Stories Book
Everything® Fairy Tales Book

LANGUAGE

Everything® Conversational Japanese Book
    (with CD), $19.95
Everything® Inglés Book
Everything® French Phrase Book, $9.95
Everything® Learning French Book
Everything® Learning German Book
Everything® Learning Italian Book
Everything® Learning Latin Book
Everything® Learning Spanish Book
Everything® Sign Language Book
Everything® Spanish Phrase Book, $9.95
Everything® Spanish Verb Book, $9.95

MUSIC

Everything® Drums Book (with CD), $19.95
Everything® Guitar Book
Everything® Home Recording Book
Everything® Playing Piano and Keyboards Book
Everything® Rock & Blues Guitar Book
    (with CD), $19.95
Everything® Songwriting Book

NEW AGE

Everything® Astrology Book
Everything® Dreams Book
Everything® Ghost Book
Everything® Love Signs Book, $9.95
Everything® Meditation Book
Everything® Numerology Book
Everything® Paganism Book
Everything® Palmistry Book
Everything® Psychic Book
Everything® Spells & Charms Book
Everything® Tarot Book
Everything® Wicca and Witchcraft Book

PARENTING

Everything® Baby Names Book
Everything® Baby Shower Book
Everything® Baby's First Food Book
Everything® Baby's First Year Book
Everything® Birthing Book
Everything® Breastfeeding Book
Everything® Father-to-Be Book
Everything® Get Ready for Baby Book
Everything® Getting Pregnant Book
Everything® Homeschooling Book
Everything® Parent's Guide to Children
    with Asperger's Syndrome
Everything® Parent's Guide to Children
    with Autism
Everything® Parent's Guide to Children
    with Dyslexia
Everything® Parent's Guide to Positive Discipline
Everything® Parent's Guide to Raising a
    Successful Child
Everything® Parenting a Teenager Book
Everything® Potty Training Book, $9.95
Everything® Pregnancy Book, 2nd Ed.
Everything® Pregnancy Fitness Book
Everything® Pregnancy Nutrition Book
Everything® Pregnancy Organizer, $15.00
Everything® Toddler Book
Everything® Tween Book

PERSONAL FINANCE

Everything® Budgeting Book
Everything® Get Out of Debt Book
Everything® Homebuying Book, 2nd Ed.
Everything® Homeselling Book
Everything® Investing Book
Everything® Online Business Book
Everything® Personal Finance Book
Everything® Personal Finance in Your
    20s & 30s Book
Everything® Real Estate Investing Book
Everything® Wills & Estate Planning Book

PETS

Everything® Cat Book
Everything® Dog Book
Everything® Dog Training and Tricks Book
Everything® Golden Retriever Book
Everything® Horse Book
Everything® Labrador Retriever Book
Everything® Poodle Book

Everything® Puppy Book
Everything® Rottweiler Book
Everything® Tropical Fish Book

REFERENCE

Everything® Car Care Book
Everything® Classical Mythology Book
Everything® Einstein Book
Everything® Etiquette Book
Everything® Great Thinkers Book
Everything® Philosophy Book
Everything® Psychology Book
Everything® Shakespeare Book
Everything® Toasts Book

RELIGION

Everything® Angels Book
Everything® Bible Book
Everything® Buddhism Book
Everything® Catholicism Book
Everything® Christianity Book
Everything® Jewish History & Heritage Book
Everything® Judaism Book
Everything® Koran Book
Everything® Prayer Book
Everything® Saints Book
Everything® Understanding Islam Book
Everything® World's Religions Book
Everything® Zen Book

SCHOOL & CAREERS

Everything® After College Book
Everything® Alternative Careers Book
Everything® College Survival Book
Everything® Cover Letter Book
Everything® Get-a-Job Book
Everything® Job Interview Book
Everything® New Teacher Book
Everything® Online Job Search Book
Everything® Personal Finance Book
Everything® Practice Interview Book
Everything® Resume Book, 2nd Ed.
Everything® Study Book

SELF-HELP/
RELATIONSHIPS

Everything® Dating Book
Everything® Divorce Book
Everything® Great Sex Book

All Everything® books are priced at $12.95 or $14.95, unless otherwise stated. Prices subject to change without notice.

Everything® Kama Sutra Book
Everything® Self-Esteem Book

SPORTS & FITNESS

Everything® Body Shaping Book
Everything® Fishing Book
Everything® Fly-Fishing Book
Everything® Golf Book
Everything® Golf Instruction Book
Everything® Knots Book
Everything® Pilates Book
Everything® Running Book
Everything® T'ai Chi and QiGong Book
Everything® Total Fitness Book
Everything® Weight Training Book
Everything® Yoga Book

TRAVEL

Everything® Family Guide to Hawaii
Everything® Family Guide to New York City, 2nd Ed.

Everything® Family Guide to Washington D.C., 2nd Ed.
Everything® Family Guide to the Walt Disney World Resort®, Universal Studios®, and Greater Orlando, 4th Ed.
Everything® Guide to Las Vegas
Everything® Guide to New England
Everything® Travel Guide to the Disneyland Resort®, California Adventure®, Universal Studios®, and the Anaheim Area

WEDDINGS

Everything® Bachelorette Party Book, $9.95
Everything® Bridesmaid Book, $9.95
Everything® Creative Wedding Ideas Book
Everything® Elopement Book, $9.95
Everything® Father of the Bride Book, $9.95
Everything® Groom Book, $9.95
Everything® Jewish Wedding Book
Everything® Mother of the Bride Book, $9.95
Everything® Wedding Book, 3rd Ed.

Everything® Wedding Checklist, $7.95
Everything® Wedding Etiquette Book, $7.95
Everything® Wedding Organizer, $15.00
Everything® Wedding Shower Book, $7.95
Everything® Wedding Vows Book, $7.95
Everything® Weddings on a Budget Book, $9.95

WRITING

Everything® Creative Writing Book
Everything® Get Published Book
Everything® Grammar and Style Book
Everything® Grant Writing Book
Everything® Guide to Writing a Novel
Everything® Guide to Writing Children's Books
Everything® Screenwriting Book
Everything® Writing Well Book